DA

THE JOSSEY-BASS/AHA PRESS SERIES translates the latest ideas on health care management into practical and actionable terms. Together, Jossey-Bass and the American Hospital Association offer these essential resources for the health care leaders of today.

Streamlining Health Care Operations

Streamlining Health Care Operations

How Lean Logistics Can Transform Health Care Organizations

AUDIE G. LEWIS

JOSSEY-BASS
A Wiley Company
San Francisco

Health Forum, Inc.
An American Hospital Association Company
CHICAGO

www.josseybass.com

Copyright © 2001 by John Wiley & Sons, Inc.

Jossey-Bass is a registered trademark of John Wiley & Sons, Inc.

AHA press is a service mark of the American Hospital Association used under license by AHA Press.

Jossey-Bass books and products are available through most bookstores. To contact Jossey-Bass directly, call (888) 378-2537, fax to (800) 605-2665, or visit our website at www.josseybass.com.

Substantial discounts on bulk quantities of Jossey-Bass books are available to corporations, professional associations, and other organizations. For details and discount information, contact the special sales department at Jossey-Bass.

We at Jossey-Bass strive to use the most environmentally sensitive paper stocks available to us. Our publications are printed on acid-free recycled stock whenever possible, and our paper always meets or exceeds minimum GPO and EPA requirements.

Library of Congress Cataloging-in-Publication Data

Lewis, Audie G.
  Streamlining health care operations : how lean logistics can transform health care organizations / Audie G. Lewis.
      p. ; cm. — (The Jossey-Bass/AHA Press)
  Includes bibliographical references and index.
  ISBN 0-7879-5503-5 (alk. paper)
  1. Health services administration. 2. Business logistics. [DNLM: 1. Delivery of Health Care—organization & administration—United States. 2. Efficiency, Organizational—United States. 3. Delivery of Health Care—economics—United States. 4. Quality of Health Care—standards—United States. W 84 AA1 L5988s 2001] I. Title.
  II. Jossey-Bass/AHA Press series.
  RA971 .L45 2001
  362.1'068—dc21   2001000577

first edition
HB Printing 10 9 8 7 6 5 4 3 2 1

CONTENTS

PREFACE

Many people are wondering what the future holds for America's health care industry. On the one hand, costs are spiraling out of control, and profitability is almost a distant dream for an unprecedented number of health care organizations. On the other hand, America still maintains the most impressive patient-treatment infrastructure in the world. Doomsayers contend that socialized medicine is the only answer and predict that the transition into such an era of health care is only a matter of time. Other, more optimistic, leaders contend that events will soon change and legislation—whether the accomplished Balanced Budget Act (BBA) or the probable governmental bailout of the Social Security Program—will serve to save the industry from continued losses and disruption.

The truth is that neither scenario is likely to affect the viability of the industry in the next decade. Health care organizations will likely face even more struggles than they have dealt with to date, unless leaders at every level begin to implement the kind of change that has occurred in other highly technology-dependent industries. The type of change needed is not at the surface level seen to date, as with cutting staff and trimming budgets. In medical terms, this is merely bandaging a much greater, underlying problem. Instead, deep-seated changes are necessary to rebuild the core processes needed if health care organizations are to drastically drive down cost and become efficient in every arena. This means changing the profit-robbing practices of yesteryear into the lean business practices needed today, in order to regain the level of profitability that guarantees all of us the ability to continue to enjoy the best health care in the world.

The chapters in this book focus on the aspects of health care that require immediate change. Most of what is written here is based on the core principles embodied in "lean logistics." As used here, the term primarily refers to the systematic process of removing waste and inefficiency throughout the purchasing, supply, distribution, and business operations chain. To this end, the book focuses heavily on showing health care executives and other leaders how to improve business operations so that reimbursements and revenue are protected to the fullest extent possible.

Finally, *Streamlining Health Care Operations* strongly emphasizes the employee side of business improvement. In truth, no remedy or plan for business turnaround can be successfully orchestrated without taking into account the critical dynamics of individual employees. The elements and principles contained in the field of lean logistics needs to be bred into the very heart and soul of employees throughout the industry so that everyone can benefit from a renewed health care business environment.

March 2001   Audie G. Lewis
Cape Coral, Florida

ACKNOWLEDGMENTS

Those who are familiar with my other books know that my wife, Heather McPherson Lewis, has always been an integral part of every work I have created. I have the unique privilege of being married to not only a wonderful woman but an excellent freelance editor as well. As usual, she has worked tirelessly to prepare this book for publication. Many thanks go to Heather for her presence on these pages.

In any work of this size, there are always countless people who have played a part, both in a primary sense and behind the scenes. This is true for this book as well. I would like to thank Richard Muhlhauser, the president of Profit Line, for his help with the business office chapter. His comments and input were much appreciated. Likewise, the staff at Neodyme Technologies provided valuable input into service-related cost issues nationally. Additionally, Joe Smith, the president of National Health Care Logistics (NHCL), contributed to this work as well.

Also, I would like to thank the wonderful staffs at the American Hospital Association (AHA) Press and Jossey-Bass for all the support and effort that it takes to bring a book to market. I especially want to thank my editors at the two houses, Rick Hill and Andy Pasternack respectively, for all their advice and work in making this project a reality.

Finally, I am most interested in hearing from you, the reader of this book, as your comments and ideas can help all of us improve the health care industry. Please e-mail me at audielewis@earthlink.net with your insights or concerns, or if you are interested in receiving other information about cost-cutting initiatives and ideas on industry improvement.

To the three best sisters
that anyone could ever hope to have:
Kathy Penrose, Debra Vos, and Brenda Pochon

ABOUT THE AUTHOR

AUDIE G. LEWIS is president and chief executive officer of Audie Lewis Consulting, Inc., a national research and consulting firm specializing in cost cutting, business improvement, supply chain analysis, and Internet projection and growth for the health care industry. He is the author of several books, including the American Hospital Association's best-selling *The Year 2000 Health Care Survival Guide*. His firm publishes the independent Mark of Excellence reports, which identify best-in-class manufacturing and service products within the health care field. Lewis is a popular speaker, and his articles and interviews have been featured throughout the industry. He has consulted to the United Nations, many state hospital associations, and other well-known health care entities.

While teaching at the Massachusetts Institute of Technology, Lewis was involved in research in streamlining logistics operations while maintaining high quality and cost parameters. He holds an MBA and an undergraduate degree in technology management. Before retiring from the U.S. Army as a commissioned officer, he held a variety of logistics positions, including command of a large supply and maintenance unit and many other critical jobs in both the medical and nonmedical arenas. He and his wife, Heather, currently reside in southwestern Florida with their four children, Maggie, Alex, Max, and Holly.

Streamlining Health Care Operations

CHAPTER 1

Introduction

Other than the nation's disenchantment with government and politics, health care stands alone as an area of disgruntlement and dis-
appointment. Whereas the medical field and associated technology available
are unprecedented, the actual organizational problems and archaic business
methods found within the health care industry have served to infuriate the
populace. The cost of health care, as well as the inefficiencies, lack of adequate access, perception of mediocre treatment, and lack of control or caring has served to make health care a blemish among other outstanding
industries.

This of course did not come about overnight. History has produced an
industry that is all too accustomed to receiving much too much compensation for services rendered. Now, in a day that calls for cost cutting and
other efficiencies, desperate health care providers are filing bankruptcy in
record number, claiming that it is "impossible" to find the revenue to stay
in business.

Of course other industries have somehow been able to streamline their
practices and do so with incredible profit margins. Should health care not
be able to do likewise? The answer is a resounding yes, and this book points
the industry toward that end. The pain of the process will be in embracing
methodologies which are untraditional within health care, and which cause
the entire organization to stretch and change. This may be the most difficult of tasks, but certainly not impossible. The tendency to hope for the
"good old days" will only serve to further the ridicule and inefficiencies of

the industry. To read this book is to look at running health care differently. To apply the ideas proposed will cause an organization to thrive and become an industry leader.

Every health care organization is going to have to learn how to effectively balance costs, quality, and patient access to great care. The health care field has long been a cost-plus industry that was able to pass total cost onto the patient or third-party payer. This climate of cost-plus no longer exists financially; however, much of the infrastructure within this industry has not yet adapted to these changes. The last few years have seen many attempts to cut staff, services, and other "unnecessary" cost in order to remain viable. These practices have undermined opportunities to get at the "real" costs of health care. Patients want and expect superior health care service and do not want nurses and other staff members cut in order to continue to receive basic health care services. Health care consumers also want and expect to continue to receive the best practices of medicine available, both technologically and clinically.

Patients want and expect superior health care service and do not want nurses and other staff members cut in order to continue to receive basic health care services.

The truth is that the health care industry does not lead the other markets in any business practice except patient care. The best business practices nationally and internationally occur outside the health care arena. For instance, the health care industry uses a model of distribution logistics that has not been used in other industries for over twenty-five years. The health care model consists of multiple layers of redundant warehousing and inventory holding layers that are costly and inefficient. In contrast, companies in the retail and food service industries, such as Wal-Mart or Publix, use a very streamlined form of distribution logistics that is very cost effective and timely. As this example shows, what is needed in the health care industry is a careful rebuilding of the infrastructure to reflect the best practices of business enterprises worldwide.

This restructuring of the industry will alleviate the real unnecessary costs associated with the industry and allow quality services and professional staffs to be supported financially.

The best business practices nationally and internationally occur outside the health care arena.

RESISTANCE TO CHANGE

Despite evidence of the need for change, there still remains an undercurrent of strong resistance to change within the health care industry. Many people may still be holding on to the hope that conditions will revert to what they were years ago, when third-party payers paid whatever was required of them. To these people, relief actions aimed at the Balanced Budget Act (BBA) and other similar legislative initiatives are paving the way back to profitable margins, where health care providers are paid based on service rendered (even when rendered carelessly). Unfortunately, these hopes will prove to be false, as the inroads of the BBA and possible relief actions are likely to have little effect on the long-term viability of health care.

The problems facing health care will not go away as a result of modest incremental changes in reimbursement trends within the industry. Such hope is unfounded because it ignores the real differences between the health care industry and others (even those closely related). The health care industry is losing ground in profitability because inefficiency and waste abound. Even casual comparison of health care business practices with those of other industries reveals hundreds of major variables that are archaic, costly, and unjustified. The entire infrastructure of health care is affected by many of these profit-robbing practices.

Part of the resistance to change in the industry springs from the hopelessness that some leaders feel in not being able to deal with the degree of change needed. Many leaders undoubtedly feel inadequately equipped to grapple with the issues and therefore choose to ignore the problems altogether. This is not an uncommon response to an overwhelming situation; even in battle, soldiers have been known to fire blindly into the approaching

Even casual comparison of health care business practices with those of other industries reveals hundreds of major variables that are archaic, costly, and unjustified.

enemy mass, because they feel over-whelmed by their immediate circumstances. Unfortunately, shots fired without aim rarely hit a target. So it is with leaders who are ill equipped to deal with the change needed within the health care industry today. Many will discover that the experiences and education of their past do not help them solve the issues of the present.

Finally, many resist change because it is frightening, difficult, and tiring. Most employees (including managers and other leaders) do not like having to learn new methods or change historical practices. People tend to gravitate toward what they know and are accustomed to. Likewise, work routines and daily functions become habits that are not easily discarded by anyone. Health care industry change spells discomfort and unrest. Organizations needing and wanting change have to understand and cope with the underlying issues of resistance that are present among both the leaders and the employees.

ACCOUNTABILITY NEEDED

Although there is no shortage of customers for health care organizations for today or tomorrow, patient health care needs must be met cost-effectively if we are to sustain the viability of the industry. Currently, many health care organizations are experiencing the age-old problem found in manufacturing communities: the costs of production sometimes outstrip the ability of the customer to pay for the product.

The health care industry has an enormous wealth of expertise, technology, and financial resources. Unfortunately, much of the strength of the resources has not been realized yet. Old philosophies of business have not been replaced with tools and techniques that maximize strengths. In many ways, the third-party-payer practices of the past may have hindered the growth of the industry by providing financial incentives for quality health care without requiring accountability for how cost-effective it was. In this regard, manufacturers, suppliers, and other important health care partners were encouraged to provide quality support without concern about inefficient research and development costs, logistical support costs, marketing costs, manufacturing costs, or any other normal business costs.

Organizations and industries become lethargic if they are not adequately held accountable for mistakes, service or product costs, or inefficient practices. For instance, many can still remember the out-of-control costs prevalent throughout the government in the 1970s and 1980s, when most contracts were negotiated on a cost-plus basis. These contract award practices bred inefficiency and waste among defense contractors, suppliers, and other awardees because there was no disincentive to prevent waste. Contractors and suppliers were practically guaranteed a strong profit margin, regardless of the quality and efficiency of their internal operations.

In many ways, the third-party-payer practices of the past may have hindered the growth of the industry by providing financial incentives for quality health care without requiring accountability for how cost-effective it was.

This same atmosphere has prevailed throughout the health care industry and still persists today. Third-party payers have historically always been the check payers for health care supplies and equipment indirectly paid through patient care offered by the health care organization. Likewise, health care organizations have not been overly interested in the *how* of equipment production or supply distribution so long as the products arrived on time and were of high-enough quality to permit good patient care. Still today, most health care organizations only concern themselves with the reimbursement amount derived from procedures and pay little if any attention to the production cost of equipment or supplies.

This structure is costing the industry billions of dollars annually and will not change until the industry becomes more accountable and demands cost-effective measures from its critical support partners. Without a doubt, health care manufacturers and suppliers can significantly cut the costs of business if forced to do so to remain in business. Those that cannot make the changes needed to remain successful will close their doors and be replaced by new businesses that can compete in the new health care market.

WHY BENCHMARKS DON'T ALWAYS WORK

Benchmarking can be an extremely effective tool for improving performance in an organization. Usually, benchmark standards are acquired by assessing the best-practice initiatives of other organizations and then using those standards as reference points for comparison and improvement for everyone else. The key to successful benchmarking is to make sure that the standards used as reference points represent the best practices to be found. One of the greatest problems with benchmarking in health care is that most of the standards have been borrowed from other health care institutions. Unfortunately, the health care industry uses some of the worst business practices to be found in the marketplace. Therefore benchmarking against mediocre or substandard performance levels found within the health care industry only brings an organization to that particular level. On the other hand, benchmarking against superior performers serves to raise business practices.

The key to successful benchmarking is to make sure that the standards used as reference points represent the best practices to be found.

To stop a continuous cycle of bad performance, it is critical that health care organizations start benchmarking as many practices as possible with the best-practice leaders in other industries. Here are a few of the market leaders in eight important areas of business:

Common Benchmark Leaders

Marketing:	Walt Disney
Quality control standards:	McDonald's
Distribution and resupply:	Wal-Mart
Inventory control:	Publix
Preventive maintenance:	UPS
Quality and low cost:	Southwest Airlines
Research and development:	3M
Internet projection:	Amazon.com

Any organization wishing to improve standards derived from these industry leaders and others like them has many challenges and changes, and undeniably notable improvements. By setting such high standards of performance, the health care industry would be on the road to a much better standard of benchmarking.

WHAT IS NEEDED FOR GROWTH

Profitability and growth will not return to the health care industry until the dynamics of cost cutting and efficiency building extend to every arena within its environment. The need for this industry to embrace growth while lessening waste is apparent. Certainly the industry is receiving messages from myriad directions that this is necessary for survival. The government, insurers, the public sector, politicians, and competitive providers are all putting pressure on health care organizations to effect change and align health care costs with those in other industries similarly dependent on technology. This pressure needs to be turned toward other critical partners as well: the manufacturing, supplier, maintenance, and service support communities.

Benchmarking against superior performers serves to raise business practices.

These pressures and expectations are driving the entire industry to become more focused, cost-conscious, and creative. Likewise, everyone is becoming much more willing to accept broad business practice changes. This book addresses these issues and offers a composite of commonsense ideas and methods for accomplishing the goals of high growth, reduced waste, and all-around excellence for health care organizations and the industry.

SUMMARY

There are indeed innumerable ways that any health care organization can find to streamline and improve revenues. Enabling and educating the people who are expected to make the organization successful—which should include everyone—is the backbone of the success of this program, which touts finding efficient methodologies at every level and in every department. The challenges are great, particularly when faced with the necessity to embrace change. If understood and properly applied, change can turn an otherwise sinking organization into the next miracle of health care.

Likewise, traditional industry benchmarking should be cast aside to make room for analyzing and using best-practice methods from other industries. Since there are so few excellent examples within the health care industry, it becomes necessary to look outside the industry for best-practice indicators and ideas.

Additionally, a new mind-set is needed in the health care industry. Whereas the past blessed the industry with an almost bottomless pocketbook, this is no longer the case. Now only those organizations that are flexible enough to make sweeping changes in their way of doing business are likely to survive or be profitable. Unfortunately, many will lose ground and close their doors rather than embrace the hard changes needed for success.

Finally, it becomes necessary to fully use available resources and apply efficient means of operating. Those who fail to wake up to this new way of thinking are in for perilous times. But those willing to roll up their sleeves and make the changes necessary will find profitability and excellence their rewards.

CHAPTER 2

The Value
of the Employee

Recent years have seen a preponderance of employee layoffs in an effort to positively affect the bottom line of many an organization. Certainly the health care industry is prone to this type of solution, given the increased budgetary constraints that were once not even a factor in health care delivery. Although layoffs may sometimes seem the only solution, creative organizations can frequently avoid such unfortunate remedies through using their current employee base wisely. Aligning the employee base with the strategic objectives of the organization requires a good deal of human resource expertise. This chapter examines how a moderately motivated employee base can be challenged and called upon to help an organization save money, solve problems, increase revenue, and succeed against the competition.

THE COST OF EMPLOYEE LAYOFFS

Organizations around the world have been finding over the last few years that massive employee layoffs and slashed budgets do not always translate into increased revenue or improvement in the bottom line. Instead, many of the sometimes arbitrary fix-it strategies end up slashing revenues as much as costs, thus resulting in no real gain in productivity, market share, profitability, or any other common indicator of business improvement. The truth is that many of these strategies are extremely shortsighted and end up creating false representations of future growth. Quick-fix methods may appease the stock market or local stakeholders for a period of time. Eventually, however, the lack of improvement to the business shows up in bond ratings or share prices that are lower than before.

Business development and growth issues are complicated and must be approached from a quantitative and commonsense perspective that takes into account the numerous interconnected dynamics present in most business environments. This is especially true for the health care industry, in which quality patient-care delivery issues present unique challenges for providers. Careful analysis and research is needed to correctly identify the critical links between proposed budget cuts and the revenues they support. Mistakes in analysis often lead to erroneous conclusions, failed cost avoidance initiatives, and further missed opportunities for correcting poor performance.

Employee layoffs and slashed budgets do not always translate into increased revenue or improvement in the bottom line.

Poor business performance is often a product of missed market opportunities. Often, the problem is not that the employer has too many employees but that the health care provider has not properly aligned itself in the marketplace. Missed market opportunities usually trigger poor economic conditions, especially if the employee base migrates to a growth-oriented competitor.

Poor business performance is often a product of missed market opportunities.

As stated earlier, when businesses cut employees to improve performance they frequently cut just as much revenue from the budget as they do cost. This is so because the majority of employees affect both outcomes about equally. This is not to say that some employees should not be cut from the staff. In fact, poorly performing employees may actually cost health care providers much more money than they save, and in some cases cuts are necessary. But poor performance is not the norm. Most workers do give their employers valuable service that is worth more than their total salary, taxes, and benefits. If this is the case, then why do so many health care providers often find themselves in the red, thus making employee layoffs appear necessary and prudent?

Part of the answer is that most employees are operating at less than optimum because the organizational leaders have not correctly aligned mission performance with the correct long-term strategic goals. Strategic goals that are out of line with the marketplace cause everyone in the organization to waste resources, miss critical opportunities for growth, and allow competitors to win time after time. An organization that is several percentage points in the red can be turned around sharply by readjusting the mission to correctly align with the marketplace. This ability to turn individual businesses around in a short period of time has been demonstrated by leading companies such as Chrysler, GE, Microsoft, Taco Bell, and others. In each of these cases, a key leader was able to redefine the internal mission to fit the realities of a changed marketplace.

If it is true that employee layoffs frequently affect revenue and cost equally, then what is the benefit to the organization or community in laying off employees? In this type of scenario, the bottom line remains virtually unchanged, except that both revenue and cost are lower. The health care provider continues to lose money and market share. In this case, it would be better to maintain the current marketplace, keep the employee base intact, and at least provide the community with a valuable service during a period of marketplace realignment.

As an example of this process in action, consider the effect of a 5 percent employee reduction on a typical hospital's operations. First, examine the business office function. Assume that a 5 percent reduction results in only one employee being cut from the business office staff. Now, if that employee was a poor performer, then a reduction in staff might actually improve the operation, or at least not worsen it. But suppose this employee represents a normal worker with an acceptable work ethic and average productivity. What effect comes about as a result of this employee being let go?

It can be assumed that there are small changes in virtually every arena that this employee affected. For instance, preadmission activities and research decrease slightly. There are likely to be small changes in the productivity of invoice processing, claims filings, late payer follow-ups, credit checks, insurance adjustment contact, lien filings, and other everyday business functions. What is the likelihood that all of these small changes do not affect hospital income in some fashion? The probability is high that there is actually a net loss to the hospital resulting from this one employee being laid off. This type of scenario can be found throughout the health care arena.

This is not to say that there is not wasted employee effort within the health care community. Many health care providers suffer from redundancy of employees' work efforts. In many cases, the redundancy is caused by mergers and acquisitions or similar growth activities that have not been correctly rolled together to eliminate wasted employee effort. But even these instances of employee overlap can often be remedied by in-house retraining efforts orchestrated by the HR department or other training and job realignment resources. Examine Table 2.1, a list of typical health care employee positions and their related cost-avoidance missions, which are often not evaluated in employee layoff plans and thus end up costing institutions more money than expected.

MORALE AND MOTIVATION

There is probably no larger crippler of productivity in the business community than lack of positive morale and internal motivation among employees. Employees perform work activities every day at varying energy levels and degrees of commitment. In most instances, the daily activity level is directly proportional to the enthusiasm and excitement they feel about their job, employer, boss, coworkers, and mission. If morale and motivation are low, then output is low, whereas if these two factors are high, productivity is likely to be high as well. In reality, morale and motivation are a measure of output. An employee who is 80 percent motivated is performing 20 percent below peak performance. In many organizations, the entire workforce is performing at this level or lower.

Streamlining Health Care Operations

Table 2.1. Employee Layoffs: Benefit or Cost?

Job Title	Hidden Cost
Biomedical engineer	Outside maintenance or service contracts
Security staff	Stolen equipment, crime
Purchasing clerks	Missed discounts
Business office staff	Reimbursements, lost income, debt recovery
Housekeeping	Patient and room turnover
Nursing and technical staff	Patient referrals, lost business, training cost
Providers	Patient throughput, referral patterns, growth
Legal staff	Contract disputes, lawsuits
Admitting	Insurance claims, patient throughput
Technology assessment	Capital equipment mistakes, costs

Underperformance costs health care organizations billions of dollars annually. As an example of the reality of this cost, consider that a job normally done by four employees requires five employees to finish if each of the original four is only performing at 80 percent of maximum potential. Therefore it is imperative that leaders understand the elements of employee motivation and strive to create a work environment that maximizes each employee's ability and willingness to become an A-level achiever.

In any health care setting, there are a number of factors that affect the morale and motivation of the employee base:

If morale and motivation are low, then output is low, whereas if these two factors are high, productivity is likely to be high as well.

- Training
- Number and quality of staff
- Management support
- Pay and benefits
- Special incentives
- Recognition and awards
- Expectations
- Roles and responsibilities
- Creative energies
- Organizational goals
- Lines of authority
- Freedom of expression for employees and managers
- Opportunities for growth and development
- Types and quality of discipline
- A host of other factors that together make up the entire work environment

INTERNAL VERSUS EXTERNAL MOTIVATION

The most efficient employees in the world are those who can be counted on to do high-quality work with minimum cost. Employee cost escalates with each degree of oversight and input required. Each of these costs is variable and depends on the character, drive, and initiative of the employee and the environment in which he or she works. These variable costs include

- High supervisor-to-worker ratios
- Training time
- On-the-job injuries
- Sick days
- Absenteeism
- Employee turnover

- Daily productivity standards

- Percentage of rework

- Low-quality output or substandard work

- Countless other issues that have an impact on the cost of doing business

Employee motivation is a common denominator to all of these cost drivers. Most organizations attempt to lower these variables through external means, such as annual evaluations, timekeeping systems, disciplinary procedures, and bonus and incentive programs. The truth is that none of these external tools effectively lower cost or improve employee productivity, because each program represents an attempt to control employee behavior from the outside in, rather than from the inside out. External methods of motivation typically add just as much cost as they remove, thus making them ineffective at improving profitability or productivity.

In contrast, employees who are internally motivated want to work better, faster, and more cost-effectively; they engage whatever resources are available to improve their performance and meet the greater needs of the organization. Limitations to utmost performance can be overcome by supplying better tools, ideas, assistance, or other support mechanisms. This serves to multiply the heightened activities and lessen the overall cost of business for everyone. Here are some methods that can be used to improve morale and motivation levels in the workplace:

External methods of motivation typically add just as much cost as they remove, thus making them ineffective at improving profitability or productivity.

Improving Employee Morale and Motivation

- Eliminate unnecessary restraints and limits on creativity and productivity.

- Institute frequent and appropriate levels of recognition and reward to encourage a positive work ethic.

- Encourage open communication throughout the organization to include cross-functional areas, departments, staff levels, customers, and business partners.
- Train employees in effective intercommunication skills, team-building techniques, and other similar skill sets that complement the goals of the entire organization.
- Streamline lines of authority and approval processes to maximize the efficiency of a well-trained and cost-conscious staff.
- Create opportunities for idea-gathering exercises such as brainstorming or knowledge sharing, to maximize employee input into daily operations.
- Use appropriate incentives to reward employees for first-class effort. Incentives should be carefully chosen to encourage behavior that is consistent with the needs of the organization and of the employee and other team members.
- Solicit employee suggestions for improvement, reward, discipline, and growth.

At every level, a leader should be encouraged to implement policy, procedures, and methods that maximize the potential of every employee.

EMPHASIS ON CREATIVITY

Health care organizations spend vast amounts of dollars annually on operational issues that could be fixed or completed for far less money through cost-effective means. In many instances, cost-effective measures can be found by using the resourceful tactics and knowledge base of creative employees. A creative, cost-conscious employee can certainly find a new and original solution to solve a business problem that might otherwise require an expensive and inefficient remedy.

Most employees can be relied upon to use their creative insights to benefit the health care organization, if the work environment is correctly oriented to solicit this type of solution and thought-provoking process.

Necessity is the mother of invention, and in most instances employees rise to the occasion. This is especially true when they understand the importance of the process and are challenged to use their imagination to solve problems that were dealt with historically through purchasing efforts, employee increases, hiring consultants, and myriad similar efforts that require similar financial outlay. Instead of implementing creative solutions, most health care organizations lean toward the quickest solution—the one that involves spending money. Creative solutions often require more thought and study, but they frequently result in far less overall cost to the organization.

Cost-effective measures can be found by using the resourceful tactics and knowledge base of creative employees.

Thomas Edison was reported to claim that his creative genius was 1 percent inspiration and 99 percent perspiration. Likewise, employees can often be enthusiastically challenged to find solutions to pressing problems by engaging their minds in war-gaming activities that result in creative low-cost solutions to just about any problem.

LESSONS FROM VIETNAM

The Vietnam conflict stands as an example in our nation's history of how a poor and ill-equipped Vietnamese army could effectively outmaneuver, tactically defeat, and ultimately upset the military and strategic goals of a wealthy, well-trained, and much more powerful nation. The Vietnamese were able to do so because they relied upon the creativity of their soldiers to effectively combat the superior weaponry of the American forces arrayed against them. They knew that they could not fight a war using the

Creative solutions often require more thought and study, but they frequently result in far less overall cost to the organization.

tactics and methods of a modern, technologically sophisticated army. Instead, they relied on ingenious techniques to hide from their enemy while employing low-cost and efficient field methods to harass, mislead, confuse, and distress American soldiers.

Health care organizations can learn a lot from this astounding history lesson. Expensive capital-equipment purchases, a robust employee base, and technologically advanced business systems do not always translate into "victorious" profit margins or the "conquest" of market share. In fact, many organizations have found that nothing seems to work adequately to stem the tide of lost reimbursement and declining revenue. The problem is not one of declining health need, but rather overpriced operations that cannot keep up with governmental and private insurer mandates to lower cost. Is cost-effective health care really unattainable? Does quality really have to be sacrificed if the organization is to remain financially viable? The truth is that cost-effective and high-quality health care *is* attainable if the organization correctly aligns its resources with the realities of the marketplace. Leaders and employees must be challenged to use their creative energy to combat the ineffective costs of the health care industry.

COMMUNICATION AND CHANGE

Change, no matter how necessary, is often seen as an enemy by employees, because it represents a swarm of unknown and untested ideas that may involve solutions that the workers feel inadequate or unable to implement. People naturally fear events that change their pattern of everyday behavior. Organizations that need to change to improve operations or profitability should consider the dynamics of change as seen by the employee. The organization must prepare appropriately for the level of resistance and opposition likely to accompany a new venture.

An organization that does not appropriately prepare for this resistance often fails to accomplish a new initiative because employees sabotage the new methodology and create problems that are nearly impossible to overcome. Opposition to change can take many forms, including passive resistance, which may be more costly and less combative than open warfare.

Streamlining Health Care Operations

Among measures of passive resistance are implementation delay, road-blocking efforts, miscommunication, improperly assigned personnel, and other tactics that serve to increase project cost and the implementation time frame. For instance, a sabotage-oriented manager may decide to assign critical implementation tasks to poor-performing employees so as to ensure the least possible chance of long-term success for the project. Subsequent failure can then be openly criticized as evidence of a poor overall plan. Many otherwise sound projects fail as a direct result of change-avoidance tactics of this sort.

Opposition to change can take many forms, including passive resistance, which may be more costly and less combative than open warfare.

Change must be presented to employees as being completely necessary. It must then be continuously communicated in such a way they want to participate in the new developments. Sabotage can be eliminated by correctly identifying the probable issues at the root of resistance and outlining a course of action that eliminates or minimizes the possible ill effects of the new program. Employees must be linked to the change as closely as possible and able to clearly see the personal benefits of the change. Likewise, they must believe in their own ability to make the transition into the new arena of change. The vision of the future has to be communicated in such a manner as to clearly portray the path and direction needed if current employees are to confidently move from one path to another. Here are some of the key elements necessary in communicating organizational change properly:

Communicating Positive Change
- Involve employees in the process of defining the limitations of current business practice.
- Educate the entire organization on the demographics of the marketplace, and show the alignment of current practice and how it fits strategically.

- Keep communications open; involve employees frequently in change-oriented discussion and planning sessions.

- Be sure everyone understands his or her role and responsibility in the new change arena, and link current performance to future expectations.

- Train ahead for job skills that may be required in the new arena.

- Create a vision for the future that everyone understands and can relate to.

- Reinforce selective elements of nonchange, and carry forward as much past comfort as possible to limit the degree of change employees feel.

- Link future rewards with present growth and change expectations.

- Challenge employees to contribute ideas and positive impressions to the process.

SUMMARY

Many organizational leaders have an unfortunate belief that cutting employees positively affects the bottom line. This is rarely so (with the possible exception of eliminating truly substandard employees). The truth is that most employees add as much to the organization as they take away, thereby balancing their value with their cost. It can be argued that retaining such employees at least allows an organization to remain in the status quo, while other cost-cutting or revenue-generating activities are put into place.

A far better solution than employee reduction is to motivate the current employee base to excellent performance. Too few organizations truly understand what motivates people to perform at a peak level. Unwittingly, external motivators are applied, such as a rigid timekeeping system, a high supervisor-to-employee ratio, and other methods of manipulating employees into performance. A much more effective means of energizing people is to implement internal motivational tactics. A worker who excels, whether or not supervised, can come up with a solution to a problem that is outside the job description. Communication, employee trust, and encouragement of creativity are just three among many methods for motivating a productive employee team.

Change is inevitable in today's marketplace. To gain cooperation in making changes, it is important for health care organizations to consider people's natural resistance to change and to address it correctly. Even a good project can be sabotaged by employees who decide that change is unwanted. Communication is important in these circumstances. Selling the idea of change and the benefits associated with it is an important way to gain cooperation at every level within an organization.

QUESTIONS TO PONDER

1. Have employee layoffs (past or present) been correctly analyzed to determine the total cost to the organization, including any potential, hidden cost areas?

2. Are organizational budgets set up in a way that allows total costs to be easily measured across departmental boundaries (such as biomedical repairs offsetting service contract costs)?

3. What steps have been taken to ensure that organizational objectives truly reflect current market conditions?

4. Is employee morale and motivation measured and factored into the business effectiveness model or a growth planning initiative?

5. What percentage of organizational resources is wasted as a result of poorly aligned mission performance goals? How does this affect profitability?

6. Does the average employee add or subtract from the profitability of the organization's mission? What percentage of employees are average? above average? below average?

7. Have excess employees (because of merger, acquisition, or other growth activity) been reassigned, retrained, or discharged to maximize internal efficiency?

8. Is your organization characterized by using internal employee-motivating techniques, or external ones? Which is most cost-effective?

9. What types of training and skill-development methodologies are used in the organization to improve employee morale and motivation? Are they effective?

10. Does a creatively oriented environment that maximizes the resourcefulness and cost-conscious attitude of employees characterize your health care organization?

11. How well does your organization communicate change to employees?

CHAPTER 3

Access

An Elusive Paradox

Q uality access is not a reality in most health care organizations. Unlike other service industries that strive to meet customer satisfaction goals, health care frequently maintains a substandard regard for customer access. This is manifested in long wait times, lack of follow-up servicing, little marketing of products or services, and various missed opportunities for business growth. By studying other service industries and by examining the health care organization programs that are breaking ground in access, it is possible to design and capture a larger market and better serve existing customers.

This chapter outlines the necessity to decipher precisely who the customer is, how to best serve this customer for efficient access, and how to reach out in innovative ways to create new access opportunities. It also examines properly using available technologies such as the Internet as well as reaching out into the population to serve potential customers through innovative programs, thereby encouraging them to become repeat customers.

DEFINING THE CUSTOMER

Before a health care organization can begin to tackle the problem of access appropriately, it must first define and segment customer groups by category of entry into the delivery point of service or care. Entry points and access methods vary greatly from one service provider to another and often translate into long waiting periods, confusing treatment costs, and unreliable reimbursement claims. Therefore, knowing the customer group and designing an appropriate entrance into the health care environment is critical.

Problems related to access are made worse if the solution is developed for the wrong customer group. For instance, the primary customer group of a cardiac catheterization lab is physicians rather than patients. This can be readily seen by analyzing the flow of patient entry into the system. Patients do not normally request a cardiac catheterization. Rather, they normally enter the cath lab system from an emergency situation, or a referral based on a prior visit for some related problem (say, chest pain). Since the primary customer is the physician, it is highly likely that subsequent patient satisfaction goals will be met primarily through a successful and timely procedure. In the same way, a child patient's parents or guardians are the primary customers within a pediatric outpatient setting since the parents' or guardians' likes, dislikes, and concerns probably drive the selection of provider and acceptable point-of-care location.

Entry points and access methods vary greatly from one service provider to another.

As these examples demonstrate, access cannot usually be defined globally. Quality access points and methods have to be designed to maximize the ease, timeliness, cost-effectiveness, and fulfillment of the needs of the customer groups represented. Access issues must also be defined in terms of the freedom of movement and flexibility required to meet the ever-changing needs of the customers. Entry into one area of service often results in the need to access related services. For example, patients entering the emergency room often require lab work, X rays, and a host of other services that represent additional entry, reentry, and exit points. Each of these service access points should be examined for ease of use, cost-effectiveness, and timeliness for both the patient and the service provider.

This is a critical concept because weaknesses in any one of these access entry points can spell serious degradation in the quality of service in all of the adjoining access points. To further illustrate this point, consider the effect that the clinical lab has on the emergency room. In many instances, emergency care cannot be delivered until the attending physician reviews lab results. What happens to quality of care if the lab personnel respond too slowly to the doctor's stat test request? Or worse yet, what if the quality of the lab procedures results in misdiagnosed illness or injury? Unfortunately, the patient does not view the emergency room visit just in terms of the immediate care given by the emergency room personnel; rather, he or she evaluates the quality of care given as a result of the total experience.

Weaknesses in any one of these access entry points can spell serious degradation in the quality of service in all adjoining access points.

As can be seen from these examples, defining customers adequately is an enormous challenge for health care providers. This is true because customers are not just patients but in fact are the providers, third-party payer groups, governmental agencies, regulatory authorities, and a host of similar groups. The problem is further complicated when one considers that each of these important participants expects service and delivery options that may run contrary to one another. On the one hand, patients want to be assured that they are getting the best possible care available and that it is delivered in a caring and timely manner. But third-party payer groups want the health care to be delivered efficiently, inexpensively, and in as streamlined a way as possible.

MIXED CUSTOMER GROUPS

Mixed customer groups and conflicting priorities among the parties involved significantly complicate the equation for resolving access-related problems. In fact, a solution often requires diligent study to identify the most important customer group. Second, each remaining customer group must be studied for the correct level of attention needed to balance the equation. An effective method to combat this problem is to assign a weighted average to each customer-group issue and to deal with the corresponding problems in accordance with the overall goals of the organization.

Comparing the differences among customer groups and assigning contributing factors to each can often help in designating correct weighted averages. Employees should be challenged to correctly assign values to different aspects of customer service to capture the corresponding weight of importance to mission readiness or performance-improvement goals. For instance, in the cath lab example, the physician provider group may be valued at 40 percent of the total weight, with the remaining 60 percent equally distributed among the patients, third-party payers, and nursing and technical staffs. In this case, decisions affecting operations and expectations hinge on the input from each corresponding customer group, in accordance with the weight of its value as a customer. In a health care setting, the value of each customer's input changes with the demographics of position as a customer to each access area.

PATIENT SCHEDULING

A quick visit to your local doctor's office would lead you to believe that patient-care processes are unavoidably slow, impossible to predict, and equally impossible to plan for. Unfortunately, health care professionals seem to have bought into this false notion because the entire industry is filled with frustrated patients waiting to be seen by caregivers who are notoriously late in keeping scheduled appointment times. It is quite common to see patients waiting for an hour or more to be seen by their physician or other caregiver. Worse, many providers and health care organizations consider these circumstances normal and do little or nothing to prevent or mitigate these problems. Passive acceptance of these poor conditions exists on both sides, creating an atmosphere of mediocrity in the timely delivery of health care.

The truth is that health care can be scheduled just as adequately and punctually as just about any other major customer service event. The problem is that most organizations have never taken the time to thoroughly understand the ebb and flow of their business well enough to accurately establish a scheduling model that fits the type of patient care and provider mix represented. An extensive statistical evaluation of any patient flow process reveals hundreds of individual variables that can be quantified to predict future time events. For instance, physicians differ significantly in the amount of time spent with patients. These differences are easily identifiable and can be quantified into time periods useful in accurately predicting patient treatment flow patterns.

Even "spike" or unusual events can be adequately planned for in a scheduling model. In truth, most so-called spike events actually do represent normal patterns when measured over a long time period. For example, it may be common for a doctor's office to have one problem patient per day. Perhaps most patients can be seen within twenty minutes or less, but one patient per day requires a full hour of care. In this instance, the wild-card patient actually equates to three patients. If this additional time is planned for in the daily schedule, then the extra forty minutes of patient care becomes a planned event. This in turn is transparent to the other patients because their arrival times reflect the additional expected workload.

Scheduling such variances actually allows the majority of patients to be seen faster than expected, which creates a climate of pleasant surprise as opposed to aggravation. The goodwill created through timely patient turnover serves to increase business over time. Smart providers recognize this potential growth opportunity and constantly monitor treatment patterns and event changes in order to stay current with accurate patient-scheduling models.

LESSONS FROM A CAB DRIVER

A cab company's customer base is probably one of the most seemingly unpredictable customer groups that could be studied in the marketplace. Customer calls are random in nature and rarely occur with more than a few minutes' prior notice. Additionally, many of these customer events happen as a result of immediate flagging of cabs that just happen to be in the area.

In reality, events that appear to be random to the casual observer actually occur at a surprisingly constant rate when analyzed over a long period of time. Savvy cab companies know how to constantly trend these random events—and parlay satisfied customers into excellent profit margins.

To understand this concept better, it is worthwhile to look at how cab companies successfully predict customer randomness and deal with the issue of supply and demand adequately to maximize profits and minimize expenditures. Cab companies know that certain key events trigger the need for cab rides. For instance, plane arrival and departure schedules significantly contribute to the need for cab services. Likewise, conferences and other key business events also greatly affect customer requests. Trends exist in virtually every transportation-related event. For example, restaurants, hotels, clubs, theater districts, entertainment hotspots, and similar locations significantly feed the cab business.

Other important trend events are also present within each of these feeder variables as well. For instance, restaurants have some key nights that are busier than others. A good cab-scheduling model takes into account the many variables and allows for the differences in customer location throughout the city. Accurate predictions represent higher profits and better customer service.

Patient care is predictable as well. Industry demographics exist and can be studied by any organization to accurately establish patient treatment pathways, services, and profitable ventures. Within each service area, there are also common immediate opportunities that can be seized. Emerging trends, changing demographics, and customer needs should be constantly reviewed so that reliable predictions can be made that positively affect both the services rendered and the profits received. Here are some common roadblocks to access that should be reviewed and eliminated as much as possible from an organization's daily operations:

Roadblocks to Access
- Distance and convenience to provider care
- Number of process entry steps
- Ease, clarity, and number of access points

- Quality of signs
- Procedure or wait time
- Customer acceptance of access points
- Poor use of technology (such as websites)
- Financial and reimbursement links

TECHNOLOGY AS AN ACCESS POINT

Access can be improved in a variety of ways that do not involve new-construction projects or other high-cost solutions. One of the fastest growing access points for virtually every industry is the Internet. Many health care organizations have embraced the use of the Internet with generic websites that do little more than passively advertise their existence. Websites of this type are akin to highway billboard signs that remind drivers of the availability of a service in the immediate area. Typical websites give a brief history of the health care organization and list the types of care available. Most display pictures of the key leaders, along with a copy of the corporate mission statement. The problem with this type of website is that it significantly limits the full extent of the technology and is therefore a wasted resource.

As an illustration of the extent of this wasted resource, imagine if someone attached a high-powered engine to a chain and lowered the engine over the side as an anchor for a boat. No one would argue that the engine would adequately anchor the boat; but the engine's "highest and best" use is to power the boat. The Internet is such a tool. When used properly, it has the capability of driving business to the health care provider and linking it to an ever-expanding patient base.

Many health care organizations have embraced the use of the Internet with generic websites that do little more than passively advertise their existence.

The Internet has the capability of driving business to the health care provider.

To further demonstrate this, suppose a health care organization specializes in open-heart surgery. Traditionally, it may have derived most of its business from the surrounding community, with perhaps a small contingent of regional patients as well. Now take that same institution and link it to areas of the country without adequate open-heart surgery coverage. In this case, both the health care organization and the remote patient group benefit greatly from a partnership arrangement generated by appropriate communication. Gaining market share through Internet projection is becoming more and more common, for every industry. The health care community needs to recognize and better use this critical tool to expand market share and increase related revenues.

INNOVATIVE APPROACHES TO ACCESS

The problem of access can really be defined as the distinction between patients with medical care needs and the ready availability of providers who can meet those needs. Some might also define the problem as having the available resources to meet the patient's medical care needs (for example, financial reimbursement avenues, training, and adequate equipment). Whatever the definition, the problem for many organizations is that patients and providers are not linked together effectively, thereby creating gaps in coverage, service, medical treatment, and profits.

Sometimes a health care organization may be missing a cost-effective avenue for gaining additional business. Most hospitals have a virtual revolving door of customers who remain unaware of the many products and services offered within the health care organization. Each department and service area normally exists as an independent entity, with little interconnectivity between them unless the connection has to do with the treatment being received at the point of entry. The potential to introduce services to the customer is lost unless the hospital services are marketed in that specific location within the organization.

Streamlining Health Care Operations

As an example of this concept, imagine the number of women who visit the emergency room of a typical hospital. Some are patients; some are family members of other patients. Each woman has for a moment in time stepped into the realm of the health care organization's "store" and will be "browsing" the aisles to get a glimpse of the types of service available. Most see only what is being offered in the emergency room. Hence, when they leave the opportunity to influence future business is gone.

Imagine the difference in customer interface at a health care organization that determines to make sure every interaction with a patient or visitor represents an opportunity to showcase the latest available health care services. Compare this idea to the common practice of "end-cap" sales used in retail stores. Stores such as Wal-Mart take advantage of every available display in the store to advertise an item that a customer might want or need. Retailers have long understood the importance of displaying as much as possible to the customers as they stroll through the store in search of some other item. Health care organizations could greatly benefit by borrowing from this common business practice.

Retailers have long understood the importance of displaying as much as possible to the customers as they stroll through the store in search of some other item.

Consider the impact that an organization has on its own future growth if leaders identify key traffic areas and access entry points and establish marketing and education programs in those areas. If an emergency room waiting area is equipped with a kiosk that educates women on the importance and availability of mammography screenings, women waiting to be seen by emergency room staff can keep themselves occupied with learning something of interest to their own health instead of just biding time reading a magazine or newspaper.

The idea of reaching potential clients through education should be greatly expanded in the health care industry. Flyers describing various diseases and treatments are quite readily available, but there is little use of other media potentially valuable in educating clients about available services. Waiting rooms and recovery rooms are a good example of wasted time and potential outreach. Instead of blaring the latest soap opera or news broadcast, the provider could be educating the clientele on the latest hospital technology or service. By way of a media department's ongoing hospital television broadcast network or simply appropriate use of a VCR, many potential clients could be reached.

Public education can also be explored and offered to increase interest in the health care provider. Holding public health forums or lectures is a means of involving the public in using the health care provider's services. Simply familiarizing people with the hospital environment, allowing them to meet or interact with caregivers, and educating them about the services available are all good ways to grow a customer base.

Promoting other health care services can actually target improving the long-term health status of the patients by making sure they are educated about health-related issues while visiting their local provider. Education can be adapted to each type of patient. Men can be encouraged to read about prostate cancer or offered a quick miniclass on the subject. Library resources and pamphlets can be made readily available and distributed during waiting periods. Professional education staff can visit patient rooms to conduct one-on-one discussion on important preventive health measures that promote long life and cost-effective health care.

Other industries make good use of these important opportunities as well. Airline companies, for example, routinely provide in-flight magazines, which serve to impart useful information about the flight itself but also information about other key destinations for future trips. Many airline companies partner with other transportation and service providers to help cement the current bonds even further. Car companies and hotel chains frequently offer programs that earn frequent flier miles when used in conjunction with air travel. There is in fact no end to the ideas that can be borrowed from other successful industries in educating present and future health care customers about the valuable services available to them.

Potential access can also be multiplied by implementing some customer service follow-up routines. Customer service representatives can place follow-up phone calls or write letters to health care clients with several purposes in mind. Checking on the patient's degree of satisfaction with the health care experience gives the provider a good indicator as to how the entire event is perceived. Any associated problems, such as settling a claim, can be discussed and potentially remedied. Additionally, a prospective follow-up service that may be appropriate to the customer can be reviewed. The customer service representative can also explain numerous health care services that may affect the general health and well-being of the customer and his or her family members. This simple method of reaching out to the patient/customer can also aid in building a sense of goodwill and loyalty toward the health care provider.

Access can also be improved by taking the services to the customer.

Access can also be improved by taking services to the customer. There are many ways to do this cost-effectively, without reverting to high-cost construction projects. In many cases, cost-effective health care measures can be delivered using methods that are just as beneficial to the patient as they are profitable to the organization. Many tests, procedures, and preventive health care treatments can be delivered to large customer groups in a high-impact, low-cost way.

One of the most effective ways to maximize customer participation in new care is to take the health care service directly to a high-traffic area. For instance, a shopping mall can be a great location for setting up an immunization site to prevent the spread of seasonal viruses such as the flu. The operations can be open to regular patients or cash-only customers. This type of "draw" site can also be set up to reinforce other preventive treatments, such as blood pressure checks, cholesterol checks, and a host of similar tests.

Health care services can also be carried to retirement communities. Opportunities abound to link to other organizations to reach a broad and stable health care community. Oftentimes, a visit to a neighborhood and community area results in future loyal customers. Many tests and procedures can be successfully carried out using portable devices, mobile vans, and similar resources.

Extended operating hours can also improve patient/customer access. In the case of breast cancer screening, many working women would appreciate late evening or weekend access. Clinics that are open in the evening and on Saturdays can increase revenues for the clinic and also lower the cost of owning expensive capital equipment through better utilization of existing services. Use this list of additional access points to supplement traditional methods of access:

Innovative Access Points
- Kiosks in local malls and high-traffic areas
- Mail-order pharmaceutical services
- Interactive Internet sites
- Newspaper supplements
- Bus, van, and transport services
- Health care referral services
- Community education lectures and screenings
- Price incentives and promotions on services

SUMMARY

The potential for health care providers to successfully serve their clientele is often undermined by the provider's ability to offer adequate medical access. Rather than accepting this as a sad reality for health care, an organization should take a proactive approach in addressing the issues surrounding access. As with other problems within health care, there are many excellent ideas and examples of how to overcome the access problem, whether within health care or another industry.

Of first importance is examining the variety of customer groups that an organization must serve and satisfy: patients, caregivers, insurance providers, government entities, and so on. Obviously, each interest group would like to be considered most important to a provider, with its various needs being of paramount importance to the organization. In reality, expectations are rarely optimally met for any of these customer groups. Organizational goals must take precedence in meeting the needs of each group, with weighted averaging being used as a good tool for reaching the best mix of customer satisfaction.

Access is also directly linked to effective marketing of the health care services available. Missed opportunities to reach potential clientele are an unfortunate problem, but one that can be remedied through a multi-pronged approach to increasing access. Making informational or educational materials available in the various waiting rooms is a good method to gain interest in the variety of medical services available within the health care organization. Taking advantage of promoting health care within the community can be accomplished in countless ways; mall booths and kiosks, educational seminars that put the public in contact with the organization, outreach to retirement communities, and mobile services all increase market exposure. Basically, being adaptable to community needs and designing an appropriate outreach program is an effective means of developing the customer base and access.

Patient scheduling is an unfortunate problem within many organizations. This need not be the case, particularly since even unpredictable industries have found methods for meeting customer expectations for timely service. Trend studies and statistical analysis are underused in the scheduling process. By incorporating these useful tools, the organization can effectively implement a relatively smooth scheduling plan, to best serve the customer and provider alike.

Emerging technology is a mostly untapped resource for additional access within health care. Using such well-documented tools as thoughtful website design to reach potential clientele is only beginning to be used effectively. The Internet should be used to its full extent to capture emerging markets, which are at times outside the traditionally regionalized health care market.

QUESTIONS TO PONDER

1. To what extent have customers been adequately identified within the health care organization?

2. Are the customer groups active in contributing ideas for improvement? Why or why not? Can this be readily changed?

3. In what way are customers measured in terms of the importance of their input to the organization?

4. Is some type of weighted average used to measure the effectiveness of decisions? If so, has this helped eliminate conflict of interest?

5. Are access points easy to identify, maneuver through, and exit from? How many methods of access are available to customers?

6. Are individual departments linked together to showcase other health care service offerings? If not, why not?

7. To what extent does your organization take health care services directly to the customer? Does this primarily involve construction or other long-term encumbrances? Are such undertakings effective?

8. How effective are the scheduling models used within your organization? What do patients think about the average wait time to be seen by their primary caregiver?

9. What percentage of current business is derived from nontraditional access points? Is this percentage on the rise, or declining?

10. Does your organization use the Internet as an effective access tool? If so, how? If not, why not?

11. Does your organization have a website? Does it offer general information, or is it used to market the business? Is it effective?

CHAPTER 4

Quality

A Systematic Approach

The health care industry is currently in a great struggle to align quality and cost. The health care of the past allowed for numerous business inefficiencies with little effect on the bottom line, whereas the present and the future viability of health care seemingly rests on everyone's ability to drastically reduce operating costs. Things look grim for an industry accustomed to expecting and allowing for the best, while reimbursements continue to fall at an alarming rate.

Fortunately, those who are willing to embrace a new way of balancing and aligning cost and quality will suffer little, if any, negative impact on the bottom line. To this end, Chapter Four demonstrates the relationship between cost and quality and outlines strategies for tying strategic process planning with tool sets needed to eliminate waste and improve operational efficiency. Likewise, the chapter explores employee-related issues affecting cost reduction and quality improvement, to further illustrate the necessity for change.

Finally, this chapter makes a strong case for balancing quality and cost against a backdrop of statistical analysis so that the health care organization can greatly improve its viability beyond even historical precedents. Instead of seeing quality degradation at the expense of drastic cost reduction, there is the possibility of reaching strategic goals by embracing efficiency and expecting superior quality.

QUALITY AND COST:
AN ALLIANCE FOR LONG-TERM SUCCESS

Many see the battle against unnecessary health care costs as a series of confrontations resulting in gains for cost reductions at the expense of quality treatment standards. For many health care providers, this is true. Leaders frequently resort to cost-cutting measures that deal with surface problems rather than the root issues that cause higher cost and lower quality. Sacrificing quality to lower cost is unnecessary and usually not the best long-term market strategy. Both quality and cost issues should be quantified and strategically aligned to gain the proper balance of cost and quality that results in optimum results.

Leaders frequently resort to cost-cutting measures that deal with surface problems rather than the root issues that cause higher cost and lower quality.

This general lack of strategic planning can be seen in the health care industry's unique historical application of new technologies and patient-care treatment methods. On the one hand, the medical field abounds with a constantly changing series of new technologies in the patient-care market, resulting from the research and development dollars that pour into the industry every year from manufacturers, researchers, governments, and a host of interested parties. On the other hand, these technologies and treatment protocols are too frequently adopted by the market as necessary patient-treatment avenues, with little regard to quantifiable justification for such purchases.

A strategy for aligning cost and quality is desperately needed if health care organizations ever hope to successfully treat patients while remaining profitable. Additionally, the entire health care industry has to dramatically improve the processes for collecting, analyzing, and strategically interpreting information about patients, providers, equipment, and other market demographics involved in aligning costs and quality. At the patient-treatment level, providers and administrators must fully understand the complexities of their own daily treatment routines so that quality initiatives can be built into each and every process to eliminate wasted effort, inefficiency, and unnecessary cost.

QUANTITATIVE ANALYSIS: TESTING FOR QUALITY IN HEALTH CARE

Many health care leaders talk about the need for quality within the industry, but how many of these same leaders actually measure the level of quality within their organization? Like cost and any other attribute of business, quality can be measured, quantified, studied, and improved by systematically monitoring performance, eliminating mistakes, educating employees and staff, and avoiding poor management practices. Every procedure related to patient treatment or the health care business carries with it innumerable inefficiencies of operation, which can be changed to produce the greatest benefit to both the patient and the provider.

Inefficiency translates into increased cost. This is true whether the issue is competency level among providers, substandard equipment, overpriced goods and supplies, poor quality control standards, or any other common variable found within the patient treatment arena.

Inefficiency often comes in the form of overindulgence as well. Some

Inefficiency translates into increased cost.

providers rely too heavily on technology as the answer to cost reduction, believing that newer is better, faster, and more efficient. This is certainly not always the case. Many times, an organization overcomplicates a treatment plan and pathway, creating unnecessary cost structures that actually reduce the profit margin. Automation is not always faster and better. Likewise, technological advances sometimes create more problems than they solve. By contrast, some technologies do significantly improve operations and lower overall cost. The key is to quantify these variables and use such measurable attributes as decision enablers to choose the best practice for the organization.

Good statistical control is critically important to this continuous process of improvement within a health care organization. Cost and quality variables must be defined adequately to predict the outcomes that any change creates in the operation of a business unit. The health care industry is a business environment just like any other, and it must be managed effectively if we are to continue supporting the ongoing mission of the industry to treat patients effectively.

Cost and quality variables must be defined adequately to predict the outcomes that any change creates in the operation of a business unit.

A profitable health care organization is better able to afford providing the best treatment practices demanded by its patient populace. Likewise, an unprofitable entity is far more likely to sever treatment plans, reduce capital expenditures, and lay off valuable employees in an effort to remain financially viable. Therefore leaders must take the time to implement good statistical control processes to better understand the strategies necessary to operate efficiently and profitably in the emerging marketplace.

Good statistical control must include methodologies for eliminating competition among partners in the health care organization. Sometimes a medical department or operating unit actually creates a quota or goal that is in opposition to the overall mission of the larger health care organization. It is important to define these potential barriers in the process and design management policy, philosophy, and communication that lessen these risks to organizational effectiveness. Employees should be challenged to question everything and not be afraid to tackle issues that extend beyond their own immediate operations. Here is a list of obstacles that health care organizations face in researching potential solutions to pressing inefficiency problems:

Common Operational Inefficiency Variables
- Inadequate training in best-practice procedures
- Unhealthy competition between departments
- Warring of political factions for scarce resources
- No understanding or use of statistical research methods
- Inadequate strategy for collecting and using historical information
- Daily operations not tied to the overall objectives of the organization
- Inaccurate documentation of patient-care events or service rendering
- No process in place to sustain continuous-improvement activity
- Limited leadership skills negatively affecting the organizational climate
- Investment shortfalls in capital equipment, personnel, and market research

Many leaders mistakenly believe that the costs of doing business are only those decided on at the organizational level. For instance, a purchasing manager may ignore the number of defective items that have to be returned to a particular vendor, because this vendor pays the freight costs for the returned item and practices a policy of one-for-one exchange for defective supplies. This practice ultimately costs the purchasing manager a lot more because in the end the organization pays for inefficient production operations. These additional costs are passed on to the customer through the higher prices that must be charged for each individual product ordered. As this case demonstrates, it is unwise to ignore the extra price paid when purchasing goods and equipment from vendors and suppliers that operate inefficiently.

In this example, a statistical analysis of operating costs is likely to reveal the number of defective items returned to the vendor and help the leaders select the best source of supply to eliminate unnecessary costs to the organization. There are thousands of similar decision processes that health care organizations can statistically measure to improve control of the variables that affect quality and cost. Each variable discovered and minimized represents a stronger profit margin for the organization and a greater opportunity for continued successful operation in the future. Here are tools commonly used to track variance in business operation:

Statistical Collection Tools

Pareto or priority charts	Scatter diagrams
Quality-control charts	Census information
Statistical analysis	Flowcharts, time charts
Financial success indicators	Inventory control data
Comparative analysis	Histograms
Utilization studies	Process improvement

Health care leaders and regular employees should be thoroughly trained to use tools such as these to improve quality and eliminate waste.

EDUCATION AND TRAINING: THE "ENABLING" ARM OF QUALITY

The medical industry abounds with intelligent, well-educated people working daily to improve conditions for their patient populace. The problem is that most of these well-educated people know nothing about the statistical process or data-collection procedures needed to determine the root cause for poor financial performance within their area of responsibility. Many health care organizations continue to operate under archaic business practices that are slowly driving them into financial ruin. Countless health care businesses continue to close their doors every year, not because they couldn't deliver quality health care

Many health care organizations continue to operate under archaic business practices that are slowly driving them into financial ruin.

but because they couldn't deliver *cost-effective* quality health care. There is a big difference.

Many of these failed enterprises could have been successful if the employees had been given the tools and education to analyze their operations correctly. Leaders often believe that only a few key people need to understand the numbers to combat ineffectiveness at the organizational level. The truth is that most of the issues affecting long-term cost are misapplied at the most basic level of the organization. Nurses and doctors and secretaries and technicians and supply clerks and many other employees greatly affect cost within the organization. It is at the operational level that employees need to understand how their jobs influence the bottom line of the organization. Unfortunately, most health care leaders never empower or educate employees to combat inefficiency at their level of the organization.

Most of the issues affecting long-term cost are misapplied at the most basic level of the organization.

To change this scenario, it is critical that leaders throughout the industry adopt a plan for involving their entire employee base in the challenge of lowering costs and improving operations. This process is best handled by proactively educating them in the skill sets necessary to recognize the root causes of waste and inefficiency. The trouble is that most ineffective operations do not appear to be ineffective on the surface. It is only by applying statistical process and stringent cause-capturing methods that employees begin to see the elements of waste that are hidden in their everyday activities. Additionally, leaders must be proactive in removing departmental and other work-related barriers to facilitate this fact-finding process.

Leaders often erroneously believe that nonbusiness-oriented employees cannot be trusted to identify and correct operational problems. This myth has been debunked by numerous highly successful businesses, notably Wal-Mart, Southwest Airlines, and Disney among others. Employees at every level of the organization can be trained quickly to understand and use such statistical tools as Pareto charts, flow charts, time and sequence charts, and other weapons against inefficiency. In actuality, the best indicator of success in using tools of this type is that initial training is available and their benefits subsequently find practical application. Employees who use these tools tend to reuse them once they have witnessed the resulting clarity and value in their own projects.

The best indicator of success in using tools of this type is that initial training is available and their benefits find subsequent practical application.

Training such as this also reinforces the employee's perceived value to the organization and allows the person to see firsthand how she or he can have a positive impact on organizational performance-improvement goals. Employees quickly come to realize that efficiency skills such as these help them progress further in their careers and protect them from the possibility of losing employment in the wake of organizational financial duress.

Likewise, profitable companies tend to retain and pay their employees better than unprofitable ones. These factors become more apparent with each lesson learned in helping the organization reach financial and quality-improvement goals. The problem shown in Exhibit 4.1 is common to many health care organizations (this illustration is used here to demonstrate financial-improvement goals).

The example in Exhibit 4.1 highlights several key elements that an organization might face in trying to improve financial viability in the marketplace. It also represents a type of project that is easily analyzed by an employee working in the billing department or other collection area of a hospital, if the person is adequately trained to use statistical collection tools (Pareto charts, financial analysis worksheets, comparative analysis charts). For instance, the employee could construct a Pareto chart to determine the highest priority, and subsequent priority missions, needed to improve the collection process on these bad debts. Additionally, he or she could create

Exhibit 4.1. Example of Bad Debt Recovery

Scenario

A large hospital had a history of steadily increasing bad debt that eventually rose to $25 million annually. Preliminary analysis of the bad-debt problem revealed that over 40 percent of the debt was uncollected co-pays from initial visits to the provider. Additionally, 25 percent of the debt was from middle-income families, representing medical procedures not totally covered by their primary health care plan. The hospital's previous debt-recovery process amounted to sending overdue-response billings from an automated computer system.

Approach

Statistical analysis of this problem could aid the leaders of this hospital in several arenas. First, it is highly probable that much of this debt will not be recovered. It is therefore imperative that the organization not waste a lot of time and energy on collections that have low probability of success. Within this structure of bad debt, quantifiable attributes of the probability of recovery could be used to structure a comprehensive debt-recovery program that would be both cost-effective and efficient. The second key item is that each recoverable portion should be prioritized to fit the highest and best return for the hospital. Using an approach like this to target this project would likely result in the quickest short-term gains and the best long-term return on this debt-recovery process.

a comparative-analysis charting process to determine the feasibility and cost of various methods of bad debt collection, to maximize the highest and best return for the time spent on the project.

There are hundreds of methods for tracking improvement projects such as this one. Although some charting and plotting tools are complicated to use, the majority of projects can be successfully tracked using a simple chart and process. A health care organization should strive to combat lost revenues and poor business performance by educating staff to use these valuable tools.

PROCESS AND PROCEDURE: THE KEY TO CUTTING COST

Reengineering and process improvement is a great contradiction in the health care industry today. Many organizations mistakenly believe that they have undertaken a comprehensive retooling and "waste elimination" program by embracing some form of process automation or workflow redesign being pushed by the latest vendor of choice. The truth is that the health care industry suffers greatly from mountains of bureaucratic process, technology overload, and myriad conflicting patient-treatment standards that have never been orchestrated under an umbrella of corporate strategy.

Cost and profit issues cannot be separated from each other under the banner of quality patient care. Sustainable quality patient care is not achievable unless a health care organization commits to an outright war on waste and inefficiency in both the processes and the procedures used to treat its patient populace. This war on waste must be fought in every arena within the health care environment. Inefficiencies exist in almost everything and can only be combated through systematically investigating and eliminating all variables that are not value-adding.

Sustainable quality patient care is not achievable unless a health care organization commits to an outright war on waste and inefficiency in both the processes and the procedures used to treat its patient populace.

The health care industry is not currently embracing process- and procedure-based cost-saving initiatives in a manner comprehensive enough to drive change in profitability and sustainable growth. It appears that most organizations have treated these statistically based projects as yet another superficial technique to be added to their arsenal of cost-cutting choices. This approach is much like the initial response of the U.S. automotive industry when confronted with Japanese imports in the early 1970s. Originally, all of the Big Three auto manufacturers just improved their philosophy of operation in order to off-set the new market change. It took them years to understand the full extent of change needed to compete under the new market conditions.

The same is going on in the health care industry today. Declining reimbursements and rising costs have dramatically changed the demographics of the entire industry, and most participants have yet to understand that only a radical retooling of their business practices will allow them to continue to operate in this new era in health care.

Change is needed in every arena. Physicians and administrators must work together to explore the full extent of waste and inefficiency present throughout the industry. Everyone must be willing to quantify the value of each variable so that quality outcomes become consistent with profit margins and growth. This means that the industry has to create methods for measuring efficiency and quality in how health care is delivered and in the tools used to deliver it. The next list shows critical aspects of daily operations within the industry that must be changed to stem the tide of declining quality and unprofitable health care.

Common Health Care Industry Inefficiencies in Operation

Scheduling models	Time and motion	Decision-making
Purchasing methods	studies	processes
Marketing initiatives	Standardization	Data collection and
Registration	practices	reporting
activities	Reimbursement	Demographic
Negotiation strategies	alignment	research
Workflow processes	Staff education and	Financial analysis
Leadership	training	Product development
development	Strategic	Facility construction
Logistical support	alignment	Approval processes
Pharmacy and drug	Packaging and	Planning
usage	delivery costs	Customer satisfaction
Debt-collection	Technology	Supplier management
practices	assessment	

LESSONS FROM GE: AN EXAMPLE OF STRATEGIC QUALITY

Over the last few years, Jack Welch, the world-renowned CEO of General Electric, has reshaped an entire corporate philosophy around a program called Six Sigma. The program is based on widespread use of statistical tools and extensive employee training to dramatically improve quality and drastically cut costs in order to maximize profitability. The premise behind the philosophy is that mistakes reduce profitability, lower customer satisfaction, and create unnecessary operating costs, all of which negatively affect the future viability of GE and its valuable customers.

The term *sigma* is actually derived from the statistical probability of the number of defects per million present in any given process. Six sigma signifies that there will be only about 3.4 defects per million values. The significance of accepting this philosophy becomes apparent when you consider that an average probability of three sigma would result in more than sixty-six thousand defects per million values. If you assume that most health care processes are conducted at the three sigma level, then it becomes obvious that inefficiencies and mistakes are costing organizations millions of dollars in lost profitability annually. Here are the most common sigma values and their standard deviation numerical characteristics:

Sigma Value	Defects per Million
Six	3.4
Five	233
Four	6,210
Three	66,807
Two	308,537

Welch has instituted this program to achieve strategic quality in the marketplace, with six sigma results as the long-term goal in virtually every arena. As a result, GE has had excellent success in significantly lowering production costs and improving quality on a number of manufactured products. The company has also used the Six Sigma program to tackle problems with suppliers, customers, and internal departments. The program works because everyday events, processes, human interactions, and results are quantified and studied to determine weaknesses and mistakes that hinder top performance. This quantification process then leads to thorough understanding of the actual problems affecting cost and inefficiency, thus allowing an organization to adequately eliminate these costly mistakes.

SUMMARY

Waste and inefficiency have long plagued the health care industry. Until recently, they were swept under the rug of high reimbursements and high quality. However, in the face of increased pressure on revenue and subsequent emphasis on cost cutting, quality is taking an enormous beating. Many leaders are throwing up their arms and stating that the health care industry is collapsing under the cost-driven mechanisms currently in place. Certainly, for those unwilling to adopt new methods for containing costs, this is indeed a dire time. But quick-fix solutions (which are in general unpopular and bad for business) are certainly not the answer for health care.

Health care organizations must transition into increasingly more efficient businesses if they are to survive. The right way to do it does not pit cost against quality. Rather, leaders must become strategists and experts at employing the highest quality at the most efficient cost. Areas in which to increase efficiency are found throughout most highly bureaucratic organizations. Virtually every department and procedure needs to come under the careful analysis of value for the dollar. Only if such statistical analyses are truly embraced and implemented throughout an organization can a profitable and efficient organization emerge.

A key issue for leaders to embrace is training people to become experts at efficiency and at statistical analysis within their own work method. Accepting the status quo at every departmental level is debilitating to an organization wrought with inefficiency. To change the mind-set and ability of health care workers is an important step in streamlining processes and increasing revenue across the board.

It is also important for leaders to truly understand the nature of process improvement and to be willing to embrace the hard choices and changes necessary for the workplace to truly improve. The uncomfortable process of change is frequently discarded for quick-fix cost-cutting solutions that outwardly make a difference but are often bad for business. Strategic statistical analysis is far superior to the frequently seen slash-and-patch policies enacted in desperation to save a project, a budget, or an entire department.

There are plenty of good examples of organizations outside the health care world that have successfully eliminated high cost without sacrificing high quality. Generally, upper management must commit to an entirely new mind-set for the organization and must be willing and able to empower the entire employee base to do likewise. The same could be said for the health care industry, as a host of once-viable organizations are disappearing, incapable of producing the changes necessary to stay afloat. The industry will no doubt see much more of this before the tide turns toward greater efficiency without sacrificing high quality.

QUESTIONS TO PONDER

1. In your organization, are cost-cutting initiatives perceived as quality-cutting initiatives by employees and customers? If so, why?

2. Can quality and cost issues be quantified and strategically aligned? What limitations exist that make this alignment difficult?

3. What methods are used in the organization to measure the value of patient-treatment technologies or protocols new to the market?

4. To what degree does the organization rely on quantitative analysis to test the quality of health care delivery? Are these methods reliable?

5. What role has overindulgence had in making your organization less profitable? Can these mistakes be eliminated in the future?

6. Are physicians and other primary care providers regularly included in corporate strategy sessions or process improvement projects?

7. Do barriers exist among departments, users, and provider groups that limit the profitability of your organization? If so, what is being done to eliminate them?

8. Does the organization train employees to use statistical research methods? If so, how widespread is this knowledge base? Is it used effectively?

9. What strategies or processes are in place to collect and use historical information dealing with the daily operations of the organization?

10. Does the organization routinely research other industries to discover methods for improving business operations? If so, have these methods worked within the health care arena? Why or why not?

11. Are statistical collection tools commonly used within the health care environment to improve operating performance?

12. Have reengineering efforts been used effectively within your organization? If not, why not?

13. Does the organization have a strong leadership development program? What are the barriers to making it better?

14. Are health care–related costs declining or rising within your organization? Does this reflect the average movement of costs in the industry? If not, can this be changed?

CHAPTER 5

Creativity

An Environment for Exponential Growth

An organization that taps into the creative ideas and solutions of its employee base has a greater capacity to meet the challenges of the future. This is true because of the inherently complicated issues that face every large organization, including those in the health care industry. Although it is vitally important to have effective and creative leaders within an organization, it is equally important to encourage the creative, problem-solving capabilities of the employees. An organizational leader can instill many new and impressive programs, but only the employee base of the organization can integrate the programs and solve the operational problems found at every level.

To effectively solve these day-to-day problems, health care workers must be challenged to come up with solutions. Traditionally, employees accept the status quo of how things operate. Unless this thinking is radically revised, an attitude of complacency can wreak havoc on a struggling health care organization. This chapter offers ideas on how to motivate leaders and workers to look beyond business as usual and creatively challenge how health care is delivered today.

CANVAS INNOVATIVE IDEAS THROUGH INTERVIEWS

Employees make up the greatest asset any organization has; their value is best appreciated when tapped for creative ideas to improve operations. One way to discover and encourage the creative talents within an organization is the personal interview. Personal interviews can be extremely effective in capturing employee knowledge and insights and turning them into the projects and missions needed to reach strategic goals. Interviews are most successful when organized around an agenda, which balances interviewer conversation about organizational goals with employee input as to how the goals can be reached and what obstacles exist to prevent or deter realizing the objectives.

Personal interviews can be extremely effective in capturing employee knowledge and insights and turning them into the projects and missions needed to reach strategic goals.

Interviews of this sort work well because employees most often understand the individual working environment and the roadblocks that exist at their level. In many instances, leaders are not even aware of the obstacles between organizational objective and employee action. Interviews also serve as a reminder to employees that leaders care about them and value their input. This aspect alone can be a valuable tool in developing highly motivated, goal-oriented employees.

Leaders at every level should be involved in the interviewing process to solicit valuable leads on how to improve all aspects of operation. Employee input should be sought for virtually every facet of business, even areas of concern outside of their immediate duties and responsibilities. For instance, an employee working in the purchasing department may be able to offer valuable insights into improving human resource functions even though he or she may have had no experience working in that environment. This is true for a number of reasons, primarily because employees relay their own experience of dealing with these other areas of the health care network. In other words, much of the solicited advice and opinion comes from a customer perspective, which can be insightful in identifying and fixing problem issues that may have eluded management.

Senior leaders should also be involved in the interview process, including meeting and speaking with employees from every level of the organization (not just other leaders). A thorough understanding of the problems experienced at every level of the organization can greatly aid senior leaders and managers in setting corporate goals and objectives that better fit the real needs of the organization. Goals that are closely aligned with the

A thorough understanding of the problems experienced at every level of the organization can greatly aid senior leaders and managers in setting corporate goals and objectives that better fit the real needs of the organization.

actual conditions needing attention are reached much more effectively than goals that are a loose fit. The interview process allows leaders to walk in the shoes of an employee and capture insights that might otherwise never be gained from meetings and conversations with peers and other organizational leaders.

TRAIN PROJECT TEAMS IN RESEARCH METHODS

Research is a tool that should be used to bring peace to the battle between administrators and caregivers. Unfortunately, the term *research* is overused to define an information-gathering event or loosely conducted project whose outcome is tagged as quantifiable, when in fact little actual systematic investigation has been conducted. *Webster's Third New International Dictionary* suggests the type of research that gets results: "A studious inquiry or examination, especially a critical and exhaustive investigation or experimentation having for its aim the discovery of new facts and their correct interpretation, the revision of accepted conclusions, theories, or laws in the light of newly discovered facts or the practical application of such conclusions, theories, or laws."

Imagine the difference that a project team could make in investigating and solving problems within a health care organization if the team members were trained to critically discover and accurately interpret the facts surrounding poor performance, lost revenues, missed market opportunities, or any other survivability issue commonly facing the modern health care organization.

In many institutions, either consultants are hired to investigate the performance problems or employees are asked to solve them but are given no tools or training to help them do so. Consulting organizations often hire experienced employees from the industry and then train them in research methods so that they can send them back into health care organizations to assist in solving internal problems. Consultants can end up spending considerable time trying to identify problems that the employees already know about. In most cases, the organization would be better served by training its own employees to become good researchers so that they can then devote their time and energy to finding solutions to the known problems. This would prevent wasting dollars and other valuable resources on educating outsiders to internal operations and methods.

Research methods involve a number of common procedures regardless of the school of thought that the investigating group follows. First, every project should begin with a problem and end with a solution or conclusion. The steps used to reach a conclusion typically involve some process of gathering quantifiable data in an orderly fashion, to experiment with methods for eliminating or reducing the scope of the problem. As such, research projects tend to be dynamic in scope because one problem or set of problems usually leads to another, and so the project team eventually finds that there are many actual remedies to be outlined and dealt with in solving the original problem.

As an example of this concept in action, consider the probable path that a research team might take in tracking down lost reimbursement revenues. Nationally, many health care organizations suffer from unrealized income, stemming from procedures that are performed on patients but not adequately reimbursed. This can happen for a variety of reasons, including a breakdown in the communication process of a multitiered patient-care delivery procedure or the complicated nature of continuously tracking the entire delivery of care throughout the network of providers. A research team is sure to find it time consuming and difficult to adequately track down all of the steps required to follow an experimental set of patients through the logistical and medical pipeline of the typical health care organization.

The project team may, for instance, discover that procedure codes, pricing indexes, and delivery techniques differ significantly from one department to another. Similarly, terms, conditions, and standards of care frequently differ, making it hard for clerks, administrators, and business office personnel to adequately define the full scope of care given within each department or service area. Each of these smaller problems is likely to

Electronic communications can remove some of the most formidable barriers.

generate a set of conditions and issues that needed to be researched separately. This is in fact the problem that most projects of this type present to team members.

SOLICIT IDEAS ELECTRONICALLY AND TRADITIONALLY

The electronic age has given us the opportunity to solve problems faster and more cost effectively than ever before. Employees can now sit at their desks and interact with people in the next office or on the other side of the globe. Electronic communications can remove some formidable barriers: culture, business background, education, experience, age, rank, title, location, and a host of differences that often get in the way of finding the best solution to a pressing organizational problem.

Health care organizations and many other business enterprises can benefit greatly from increased reliance on electronic interchange to further organizational goals. Employees should be encouraged to use their computers and other electronic media to gather information, ideas, and problem-solving solutions, internally and externally to the organization. For instance, common problems can be presented in a chat-room format so that employees at every level are encouraged to give their opinions and advice in solving critical issues. Additionally, they can be encouraged to present ideas at any time, even after hours, by accessing an employee website using a home computer and the Internet.

The benefit of this is that the organization soon develops a strong network of critical communication resources that help expand its profitability and delivery of patient-centered health care. The network can include the employee base itself, other health care organizations, business partners, and even patients and other customers. Even the customer base is likely to be extremely interested in giving the organization ideas for improvement. Such an information network undoubtedly becomes a strategic force in shaping the future growth and profitability of the institution.

Employees without access to electronic communications can still be included in an idea-gathering or problem-solving methodology through such traditional means as annual employee and customer surveys, interviews, brainstorming sessions, education retreats, and forums.

Technology also opens the door to a flexible work environment. The health care industry is behind others in offering employees the opportunity to work away from the traditional office environment. Allowing (and appropriately using) the virtual office can permit an organization to offer employees flexibility that few others have. The administrative side of health care particularly can benefit from integrating this creative, low-cost technological solution to any number of problems, including workspace availability, after-hours scheduling, employee flexibility, and so forth.

Technology also opens the door to a flexible work environment.

REWARD EXCELLENCE IN CREATIVE LOW-COST SOLUTIONS

Any health care organization can significantly improve its profitability and market viability by engaging employees in a veritable war on waste and unproductive activity. Employees at every level should be encouraged, through an effective reward program, to identify opportunities for process improvement, especially involving quality, low-cost solutions. Examples of excellence in low-cost and effective problem resolution should be broadcast widely to the entire organization so that everyone benefits from ideas that work. This encourages other employees to develop and offer up ideas that work as well.

Sam Walton, the founder of Wal-Mart, was well known for his ability to involve employees at all levels in the cooperative business of delivering on customer expectations while lowering overall cost. He understood the reality that individual employees can be counted on to generate common-sense ideas to routine operational problems. This fundamental truth applies to the health care industry as well. Answers often go unfound because the right people have not been involved in the process. Operational problems may not be dealt with properly either because management is not the appropriate source for a solution to the problem or because the employee base is not properly encouraged to solve operational problems.

Employee rewards don't have to be expensive or elaborate to encourage input and solutions. In many instances, a carefully orchestrated thank-you or pat on the back is an appropriate way to recognize an employee. In all probability, your health care organization is going to find that a broad range of reward devices and methods works best for stimulating valuable problem-solving input. This could include certificates for dining out, departmental parties, cash incentives, travel awards, trophies, and a host of other encouraging rewards.

USE EDUCATION AND TRAINING RESOURCES TO EXPAND HORIZONS

An organization can become stagnant and ineffective as it continues to conduct business day after day in the same manner. This stagnation usually precedes lost revenues and misaligned market penetration. A health care

Stagnation usually precedes lost revenues and misaligned market penetration.

organization can reduce this likelihood by actively involving the employee base in constant education and revitalization. Education and training in new methods, procedures, and technologies can prevent employees from getting into a rut in their work life and stimulate new ideas for competitive growth.

Organizations that adopt a constant betterment mentality and are always on the cutting edge of change and adaptability can quickly recognize opportunities for growth in the industry. On the other hand, organizations that look inward and practice archaic procedures tend to plateau and are at much greater risk from competitors. Constant training and improvement should permeate the organization. Employees should feel a sense of urgency in keeping up their skill and knowledge base so that the organization does not fall behind. Likewise, leaders should emphasize the importance of skill development and recognize employee effort in this critical growth area.

Organizations that look inward and practice archaic procedures tend to plateau and are at much greater risk from competitors.

CONSIDER INNOVATIVE PRACTICES FOR RESEARCH AND DEVELOPMENT

A creative organization is active in developing new methods, processes, and procedures that improve operations, cut costs, and create value. In many instances, health care organizations may find that they have to pave the way for the entire industry. Change comes as a result of some organization taking the initial steps to establish a new business model or innovative approach.

There are examples in other industries in which a business seems to thrive on innovation and change. 3M is widely respected for its leadership role in research and development. Its efforts are often held up as the standard for other contenders for other would-be leaders. In the case of 3M, the organization has purposed to lead its industry in developing new patents, inventions, and consumer products. To this end, the leaders developed a corporate philosophy of aggressive research and development that is far ahead of the industry standard. This corporate direction sets 3M apart and helps to guarantee the company a role in the future. A health care organization, too, can be challenged to lead the way in developing patient-treatment techniques, service entry points, and numerous other important standards for improving the quality of health care in the industry.

ENCOURAGE BOTTOM-UP SOLUTIONS THROUGH EXECUTIVE INTERACTION

A true leader has the ability to create and communicate a vision for the employee base that is readily understood by every member of the organization. It is important that leaders become adept at communicating the vision effectively throughout the entire organization. One of the best ways to accomplish this is for senior leaders to personally interact daily with employees from every level of the organization. This is a critical concept because organizational structures by nature are set up to inhibit this sort of executive-and-worker interaction. Lines of authority, supervisor-subordinate reporting relationships, and other lines of demarcation separate leaders from employees and limit any opportunity for creative interaction and growth.

Executives should fight this separation and not allow seemingly important executive activities to derail the critical function of vision emplacement. The validity of this concept can best be seen by comparing it to an illustrative practice: the kind of vision alignment demonstrated by military commanders throughout history, by which they are taught to pass on a "commander's intent" to all of the unit personnel. Everyone is able to

Leaders at every level should make it their goal to constantly educate people as to the long-term goals of the organization.

interpret the commander's wishes when faced with decisions that must be made in the commander's absence. If a soldier in battle is separated from his or her normal unit, the commander's intent serves as the mission guide. Military history abounds with heroic stories of soldiers who continued to fight against unbelievable odds while relying on their interpretation of the commander's wishes in whatever circumstances they encountered along the way.

Health care employees, too, can be encouraged to respond correctly to any given situation if they fully understand the intent of the executive leadership. Therefore, leaders at every level should make it their goal to constantly educate people as to the long-term goals of the organization. The truth is that an organization of people can get a lot more done than any one person can, and senior leaders find they can accomplish a great deal by broadcasting their message to as many organizational employees as possible on a given day.

SUMMARY

Although many health care executives would acknowledge that employees are their most important asset, few effectively tap into the creative talents of these same people. Rather, the industry tends to establish a traditional business hierarchy in which employees are trained to their particular job and not encouraged to creatively improve the general work environment. Obviously, an atmosphere of this type does little to reduce waste in the organization, nor does it allow employees a sense of well-being achieved through looking for creative solutions. Job stagnation, and thereafter organizational stagnation, is the result.

An organization wishing to begin tapping into the creative ideas of its employees would do well to begin with an internal interview process, organized to determine areas in which the employee's work can better line up with organizational goals. Identifying areas of waste and how they can be eliminated, garnering ideas for streamlining operations, and of course generating revenue are three important benefits of this interview process. Others include clarifying levels of job satisfaction, and learning what employees believe about who their customers are and whether customer service is an established goal for the employee.

Thorough research methodology should be used to combat problems within an organization. This process is generally left to a team of consultants, as opposed to using the existing workforce. Through an increase in specialized training, it is possible to obtain the best results from people who understand the processes of the organization, rather than systematically outsourcing such tasks.

Exchanging information can be greatly enhanced through better use of electronic communications. Creative ideas can be encouraged from a host of employees, customers, and others who are interested in improving organizational operation and who feel comfortable using electronic media. Any method that encourages people to creatively tackle a problem can be beneficial.

Communication plays a major role in an organization's ability to motivate employees to improve operations. Once goals are transferred to the employee base, the added incentive of an effective reward system can help to encourage creative problem solving. Additionally, emphasis on training and personal career development reduces employee stagnation and moves the organization forward.

Creativity is vital for an organization wishing to become an innovative leader. Leadership goals must be established and then communicated that allow the organizational environment to thrive on cutting-edge methods. Executive involvement is important for success in this area, just as it is in encouraging best practices throughout the organization. It should be the goal of every organization for employees to know the organizational goals and integrate them into their daily work life. Executive interaction is vital to this accomplishment.

QUESTIONS TO PONDER

1. Are interviews regularly conducted with the entire employee base? Do leaders at all levels within your organization participate in this process?

2. Do employees and leaders regularly receive training in counseling and interviewing techniques? If so, has this helped to improve the organizational climate?

3. Have organizational goals been set that include input from front-line employees? If so, to what extent was the input filtered through other leaders?

4. What type of training and skill development is offered to employees to deal with obstacles to long-term strategic growth?

5. Would your organization benefit from extensive training in common research methods? Why or why not?

6. What percentage of research projects are outsourced to consulting groups? Has this been cost-effective?

7. Does the organization rely heavily on electronic communications to conduct daily operations? If so, was extensive employee education and training included in the implementation? Has it been effective?

8. To what degree has technology allowed your organization to create a flexible working environment? Has this helped to substantially lower the overall cost of business? How (or why not)?

9. Has technology helped to erase barriers among employees and departments, and other sources of internal conflict?

10. Are employees rewarded for finding creative low-cost solutions to operational problems? If so, is the program worth the cost?

11. Would outsiders characterize your organization as cutting-edge? Why or why not? Is the employee base challenged to be constantly revitalized through education and training? Do employees have a sense of urgency when it comes to acquiring better job skills?

12. Are leaders challenged to be innovative in solving organizational problems? If so, how effective have these practices been?

13. Is senior leadership visible and accessible to employees? Has this visibility translated into bottom-up suggestions on problem solving on the part of employees? How (or why not)?

14. Does your organization have an effective ongoing training and education program for keeping the important goals highlighted with the entire employee base? What can be done to improve the program?

CHAPTER 6

Human Resources
The Critical Component

A t a time in which technology is touted as supreme, it is important to remember that without excellent employees there is very little to keep the competition from gaining ground. This is true in the health care industry—from the operating room down to the freight dock. Hiring, motivating, and retaining the best team of employees is the key to success, and it is the only hope for an organization wanting to become a leader in the industry. This chapter examines ways to reach this goal of having competent, self-motivated health care team members, even in a marketplace that may be highly competitive.

CREATE THE BEST

Open almost any newspaper in this nation and the health care industry's desperate plea for employees jumps off the pages. Hire-on bonuses, flexible hours, and countless other tactics are being used to entice qualified employees to work at one organization or another. The truth is that if an organization is truly outstanding and has a reputation within the community of being such, these tactics are not necessary. Instead, employees are pounding on the doors to get in, and recruiters have the pick of the best. Reaching this level of desirability does not happen overnight, obviously. The only way to benefit from such enthusiasm from the potential employee pool is to have a strategic plan for acquiring and retaining the best employees.

It can be argued that wages drive employees to one organization rather than another. This is only partly true. There are a great many who would trade a top salary for the best working conditions at the most reputable organization. Too many organizations forget the other motivating factors involved in choosing an employer: Is my job secure, or is the organization known for their frequent layoffs? Are there any opportunities for growth through planned training and advancement? Will I simply be a faceless employee in a sea of other faceless employees, or will I be treated with respect and encouraged to contribute above and beyond my basic job expectation?

On the strategic level, an organization must build from where it is and then begin to reach out for excellence. In other words, if the current employee base is unhappy or only marginally motivated, it is important to correct this issue before trying to build excellence through new hires. After all, the established employees pass on their standards to the new hires, and this is likely to continue any cycle of mediocrity already present.

To begin with, it is probably not necessary to hire a consultant to analyze the existing employee base. A savvy human resource manager can certainly do the research within and outside the organization to establish industry standards and receive employees' complaints or ideas for improvement. An anonymous survey of current employees could no doubt draw reams of information helpful in improving the organization and the level of worker satisfaction. This list of survey questions is just a start for any organization that wishes to effectively draw upon its current employees to become excellent:

Sample Survey Document of Current Employees

1. Why did you choose to work for this organization?

2. Does this organization meet your definition of an excellent place to work? Explain.

3. Do your supervisors listen to your ideas for improvement?

4. Are you satisfied with your salary? Why or why not?

5. Are you satisfied with the benefit plans of this organization? What would you change?

6. Are the executives of this organization in touch with the issues you encounter? Do you think they care about the level of effort you put into your job?

7. What would it take to make this organization the best in this area, a place you would highly recommend to your friends and colleagues to seek employment?

8. Do you find yourself looking at the want ads or contemplating a job move? Why?

9. Do you feel that your coworkers and supervisors treat you fairly here?

10. Are you offered the training and support necessary to do your job with excellence? Please explain your answer and identify ways of improving support and training.

It should be obvious that this type of survey works from the janitorial staff to the executive offices. It is an opinion survey that gets at the heart of employee motivation. Some organizations are in such a poor state of motivation that employees may simply ignore or throw the survey away, or answer the questions sarcastically. These are signs that there is little hope in the minds of the employee base that change will occur. Their opinions have been disregarded for so long that a mere survey garners no interest. If this is the case, it should be taken as a powerful wake-up call to the administration and executives.

After the survey comes the personal interview. Obviously, the interviewer must guarantee a high level of trust and anonymity, or else very few people will feel confident enough to be entirely candid. Communication from the highest level of the organization must guarantee that the surveys and personal interviews are to be used solely for the purpose of organizational improvement. It may be necessary to hold off-site interviews, conducted by an outside organization, to reach some disgruntled employees. Certainly, whoever conducts the interview cannot be construed as anyone with the ability to affect the job security or future evaluation of the employee.

Like the survey, the interview is simply a means of gathering motivational information from employees. Listening and learning are the key factors here, rather than sticking to a rigid set of questions. Oftentimes such an interview simply involves the interviewer writing down what an unsatisfied employee wishes to share. In a way, this is an opportunity for the employees to express themselves as they would to a friend. These interviews can contribute a great deal to the future effectiveness of the organization. Tapping into the existing motivational drives of an employee base can help to strategically realign the human resource department—and often the goals of a health care organization.

Tapping into the existing motivational drives of an employee base can help to strategically realign the human resource department, and often the goals of a health care organization.

The positive and negative aspects of an organization should become clear, whether through a survey or an interview process. It is a matter of solid communication and establishing positive change that begins a process of increasing employee motivation, commitment, and trust. Periodic follow-up surveys or interviews can serve as checkpoints for an organization on the way to establishing itself as a leader in health care.

HIRE THE BEST

Once an organization is perceived as a leader, it becomes much easier to hire the best employees. Until that time, the marketing department can play a key role in creating a positive image in the community, in addition to the reputation garnered by already satisfied employees. The added benefit that a positive marketing program brings to the potential client community can likewise motivate the best people to seek employment at a particular organization. Factors that establish the health care organization as a technological leader that is also friendly, warm, and caring appeal to potential patients and employees alike. In many cases, it is wise to spend money that is budgeted for classified want ads on a strong community marketing plan instead.

When it is time to consider new employees, the interview process can make a tremendous difference in attracting the best. All too often, the process is treated as screening, which puts the potential employee on the hot seat and rarely establishes relaxed communication. A good human resource department spends time interviewing only highly qualified employees to begin with. Screening should be done almost completely prior to an interview, thereby establishing the exact qualifications of each and every potential employee. Establishing rapport and selling the health care organization to the potential employee become the main goals of the interview process.

Of course, this methodology is completely opposite to what most people experience in the interview process. This is exactly the point. From their first introduction to the organization, typically the HR department, the potential employee can see that things are different here. The person is treated with respect, rather than badgered with questions that challenge her integrity and question whether she might be criminally suspect. In essence the message is that the candidate is, as a person, exactly what the organization needs to be: on the cutting edge and excellent. Keep in mind that HR should already be confident that this is true of the potential hire. Check the references—not last, but first! Of course, this takes time and energy, but so does interviewing fifteen people for one position when only two truly meet the high standards set by the organization.

Another common mistake in the first interview is to send the potential employee home to await a second and possibly even third interview. This usually means that the person will not meet anyone from the department in which he might work until after the initial interview. Again, this is a bad idea that wastes his precious time and conveys the message that he is not really being considered seriously.

Imagine the surprise of the interviewee if he is informed that his first interview includes meeting most of the potential colleagues and the direct supervisor. Possibly the potential hire can be taken on a tour by other departmental colleagues, or be included in something being worked on that very day. Competing health care organizations can hardly offer anything as impressive as this shining first impression. It is paramount to the success of such a process that everyone within the organization be willing to devote some of his or her time and energy to it. But this seems only natural to current employees who realize that their organization is on its way to becoming the best. Things will be different.

Generally speaking, it is possible that most of the potential interviewees will make wonderful hires. After all, if only a handful of interviews are conducted, with only the most highly qualified candidates invited for an interview, chances are high that many good people have to be disqualified. This need not be the case. Smart organizations do not let terrific, highly qualified people walk out the door, even if they must be hired for something other than what they were originally interviewed for. This means that people may be cross-trained, or fully trained from their first day on the job. This costs money. But what are the chances in a world full of mediocre players that an outstanding candidate will walk in the door every day? Health care organizations need to make it a priority in the human resource department that outstanding people be recruited. Period.

KEEP THE BEST

Employee turnover is a tremendous problem in health care. It has become commonplace for people to change positions for any number of reasons, with loyalty to an organization seemingly a thing of the past. Similarly, it is not comforting to believe that the only reason some people stay with an organization is to participate in a vested retirement plan or receive decent benefits. It is a good idea to have such plans, but it is difficult to calculate the value people are contributing to an organization if their primary reason for remaining is to retire well. In such a case, only minimum effort should be expected of some.

With this in mind, it might be wise for a health care organization to analyze ways to motivate such people to leave early. Cash incentives seem

Streamlining Health Care Operations

to work well. While downsizing, the armed forces found that a lump sum of cash was highly motivational for many soldiers who might otherwise have remained for a twenty-year retirement. One might believe that everyone will be motivated to leave if something other than the traditional retirement plans are offered. This is highly unlikely for those who are motivated by their job, satisfied with their compensation, and readily recognized for their contributions.

Intangibles are critical to success in retaining the best people.

Intangibles are critical to success in retaining the best people. Salary and benefits become only part of the reason for employee departures if people are underpaid or unfairly punished by a lack of salary increases. Organizations that are promoting excellence should rarely see a case in which full increases are not given yearly. Supervisors should be held accountable for their judgments in this area, particularly where a personality conflict rather than a competency issue may be at hand.

Psychology plays an important role in employee retention and internal motivation. Since neither the president nor the HR director can be available to listen to everyone's ideas and gripes, it becomes necessary to train supervisors of all levels on the need to listen to employees and communicate effectively. Although the executives of the organization can set reward systems in motion, implementation and enthusiasm must be found at every level of the organization to reap success. It is wise to have an open-door policy in the HR manager's office, for employees who feel they cannot speak openly with their supervisor or have a problem concerning the supervisor.

PAY THE BEST

To understand why an organization must pay the best, it is wise to consider the hiring process. If the potential employee has already been highly screened, as I have suggested, and is a wonderful prospective employee, it stands to reason that top compensation will be offered.

Common sense suggests that people who are the best will be paid the best. Keep in mind that this is the message that every employee should be receiving within the organization. The best health care organizations should be paying the best in the region. Why? Internal employee motivation is captured in the process. "We are the best" is a marvelous way to feel. It keeps people on their toes, keeps them motivated, and encourages them to find ways to improve the organization, find solutions to difficult problems, and even recruit other fine people.

Budgetary constraints cannot be completely ignored, but a good HR department can research the average annual salary of most positions and offer a certain percentage more. How can this be favorable in an industry that often cuts salaries or personnel to stay viable? The overwhelming evidence from the U.S. population suggests that health care needs are on the rise, not declining. Having too many people in the organization is rarely the problem. With people standing in line to receive the best health care, it is time to realize that offering the most outstanding service to the community virtually guarantees viability. Cost savings can be realized in countless other areas of an organization; particulars are suggested throughout the remainder of this book.

EDUCATE, TRAIN, AND REDEPLOY

An organization that treats its employees like family members retains the best people and keeps them on the cutting edge of their field of endeavor. Consider a father or mother preparing to send a child to college. Their motivation is not for their offspring to perform at a C level, but to graduate with honors and go on to greatness in the chosen area of study. Likewise, an organization that displays this level of concern and encouragement for employees reaps a strong workforce that is prepared to meet the challenges of health care in the future.

In a perfect world, the human resource department would have to conduct very little outside recruiting. After all, the organization already has talented people who can be educated and trained to continuously meet its challenges. Only if it is growing, or filling positions toward the bottom of the organization left vacant through internal promotions, should there be the need for much recruiting. Instead, like a good college guidance counselor, HR can engage in challenging people to grow and fostering the continuous progress of the current employee base.

The nursing staff is a good example. Encouraging and funding advanced training for the entire nursing staff (including college for some) allows continuous professional growth of the staff, adds loyalty and retention, and helps prevent job burnout. In other words, give bonuses of some sort to the existing staff rather than recruit new hires, and lower the costs associated with high employee turnover.

Redeploying, or moving people around the organization, can aid in employee retention and can also be used when market conditions call for an organization to shrink or grow in certain areas. Job retention does not seem to concern the health care industry, as it should. Very few organizations are sensitive to the physically and emotionally exhausting requirements of many health care positions. This leads to the unfortunate loss of many talented employees who might otherwise have been periodically relieved of their stressful job requirements. For instance, rotating emergency room and other critical care staff away from these highly stressful areas for a period of time can relieve employees enormously.

Redeploying is also useful when market conditions dictate changes in the dynamics of an organization. Strategic planning, and an awareness of area demographics, can allow an organization the lead time necessary to retrain internal employees who might otherwise have to be laid off. The costs and ill will associated with layoffs—too often followed by recruiting for growth in another area of the organization—demonstrate lack of planning, and even of caring. It is very difficult for the remaining employees to sense much pride or loyalty in their organization when poor judgment of this sort is made.

CREATE A CUSTOMER-DRIVEN CULTURE

The call for health care reform and the ensuing drive to cut industry costs seem to be alerting the industry to examine how health care is conducted, and how health care employees are trained and treated. Whether it is large or small, a health care organization's goals should center on high customer satisfaction. How well this goal is met determines the ensuing success of the organization.

Therefore, every individual within the organization should be aware of and driven to meet the goal of high customer satisfaction. Visit a typical emergency room, or most any hospital department, and it is rare to find a truly happy customer. Instead of touting a visit to the local hospital as a surprisingly good experience, most patients and their frustrated families have a long list of complaints to share with friends and relatives. They were not treated with respect, they were not told what was happening, they were made to wait for long periods of time, the food was bad, and so on. Even within the organization, it is difficult to find employees who feel that interdepartmental service personnel treat them with a high level of quality. A health care environment fitting some other description than this can be said to be on the cutting edge.

The culture of health care delivery has created an expectation of being treated much less favorably than one would wish. The culture of an outstanding health care organization should be completely different. Employees should feel they are a part of the Ritz-Carlton of health care. Consider how people are treated at an exclusive and expensive resort hotel: greeted with a smile, escorted to and fro, given the finest cuisine to choose from, never made to wait, candy on the pillow, and so on. The mental picture is what is important here, not the exact specifications of being a hotel. It is the manner in which customers are treated, the entire attitude of respect that must be conveyed, that is the goal. This is a foreign concept in most hospital settings.

The Nordstrom department store chain has become a famous example of how a pricey retailer can train employees to steal customers from the competition through customer service alone. Rather than hiring sales people at minimum wage and essentially training them as cashiers, Nordstrom trains its people to respond to customer needs. Going the extra mile to find the perfect garment for a customer is the norm for this retailer. It is common for a follow-up note of appreciation for a sale to be sent to a customer. Customers are called and informed about special merchandise or savings.

Streamlining Health Care Operations

Who wouldn't want to shop there? Likewise, who wouldn't want to return to, work at, or go to a health care organization that treated one as a person of high value? No marketing campaign can compete with this type of customer-satisfaction results.

To create a culture like this within a health care organization, customer service training must be implemented. It is also important that the executives and all managers, supervisors, and leaders of the organization demonstrate these very traits by treating the employees as their customers. Essentially, they should be the first to be trained in customer service. In other words, the vice presidents should be seen as having the same attitude toward their managers and other workers as is expected of those greeting, treating, feeding, driving, rehabilitating, and administering health care to the actual customers. Everyone within the organization must identify who his or her customers are and proceed to serve them accordingly:

- The payroll clerk's customers are the employees receiving paychecks. He should treat all paycheck recipients respectfully and promptly, apologizing for mistakes and making timely changes.

- The cook's customers are both the staff and patients of the organization. Cooks should survey their customers to find out what they most want to eat, and adjust the menus accordingly (within dietary restrictions, of course).

- The financial director's customers are those auditing and administrating the financial resources of the organization. She should be supported with the best tools to do her job and with her door open for anyone needing guidance.

- The nurse aide's customers are the patients. The aide should address a patient with the courtesy of a Mr., Mrs., or Ms. as appropriate; the aide holds the customer's high satisfaction as its primary motivation. A good goal would be to have at least one patient thank the aide daily for outstanding care, or to have one patient a day tell a supervisor of the outstanding care received from that employee.

Incentives should be part of the organizational culture to achieve high customer satisfaction. Motivation to excel in customer satisfaction is internally driven in this case. Such intangibles as pride, satisfaction in recognition for a job well done, being part of a team, and so on are the primary motivators. Undergirding this can be organizational rewards such as posting employee of the month notices, newsletter recognition for meeting or exceeding customer satisfaction goals, an annual banquet or picnic in which persons or departments are recognized for outstanding service, and so on. Each organization has its own method for recognizing outstanding attributes. Keep in mind that people are rarely praised for doing their job well, but they are frequently criticized for making an error. Praise, recognition, and rewards are great methods of motivating people toward excellence.

Empowerment within a health care setting should be seen as an opportunity for all employees, regardless of title or job description, to be given the ability and power to make changes that positively affect their way of working or meeting the goals of the organization.

Another underused method for improving an entire organization is to perpetuate the idea of empowerment. Empowerment within a health care setting should be seen as an opportunity for all employees, regardless of title or job description, to be given the ability and power to make changes that positively affect their way of working or meeting the goals of the organization.

Surprisingly, people need to be encouraged to speak up if they find a flaw in a particular job methodology or if they find a way to accomplish something better. Few people will rock the boat with suggestions for change unless it is encouraged by management and broadcast as an important goal. Once empowered, employees can then freely share their ideas for change with supervisors and managers, who should promptly implement as many suggestions as possible. With rare exceptions, calling a meeting to discuss such changes is totally unnecessary and against the entire idea of empowerment.

Empowering employees has numerous rewards for a health care organization. Certainly the cost of conducting business can be greatly reduced if the entire organization hunts down ways to trim the bottom line or bolster revenue. Creativity in these areas can work from the top down, and from the bottom up. Eliminating or streamlining unnecessary procedures throughout any organization is obviously beneficial, and most problems are undetectable to all but those doing the actual work. Empowered employees who have a customer satisfaction goal can improve customer satisfaction by changing time-consuming and costly administrative and clinical procedures.

LESSONS FROM SOUTHWEST AIRLINES

Southwest Airlines has done extremely well in an industry plagued by lateness, high cost, and low customer satisfaction. As a matter of fact, Southwest excels in the very areas that most other airlines fail in. Southwest is timely, keeps cost low, and can brag of high customer service satisfaction, outrageous employees, and an outstanding safety record.

Southwest accomplished this by purposely being different from other airlines. From the beginning, the airline determined to offer incredibly low fares, while other airlines classified people as "those who fly" and "those who don't," focusing on the former and ignoring the latter. Southwest tapped into a market of people who had never had the ability to afford flight. They did it with highly motivated employees and a can-do attitude.

Driven by employee and customer satisfaction goals, Southwest employees take personal pride and ownership in a job well done. Looking for ways to cut costs and streamline operations is part of the culture of the airline, just as much as having fun is. For the health care industry, Southwest Airlines can stand as a reminder that things can be done differently, successfully, and profitably.

SUMMARY

In a highly competitive health care market, it is important to the success of an organization to hire, motivate, and retain a solid employee base. Rather than maintain a level of mediocrity within the organization, it is important for both existing and prospective employees that a strategic plan for building an outstanding organization be implemented. Accomplishing this virtually guarantees the loyalty, growth, and retention of current employees and encourages the best new hires to seek out the organization for employment.

The first step in building excellence among employees is to analyze their motivational level. Survey and interview techniques collect information for improving the organization and making it a great place to work. The answers lie within the current employee base, and successful organizations are continuously asking employees how to make things better.

The traditional methodology for hiring employees should be almost entirely dismissed, as it invokes a negative first impression and puts the potential new hire in a defensive position. Rather, the human resource department should carefully prescreen for the best potential job candidates, and invite only the most highly qualified and highly recommended to a friendly and more involved introduction to the organization. The best organizations hire as many outstanding people as possible, even if it means immediate retraining.

An organization that wishes to retain its employees understands the various intangible reasons that people stay. Training in listening and responding skills must be implemented throughout the managerial and supervisory staff. Additionally, rewards systems need to be encouraged at every level of the organization.

It is a natural assumption that the best organizations, which hire the best employees, likewise pay the best. Paying employees well encourages them in many ways, notably instilling a sense of pride and internal motivation toward strong performance. For the most part, budgetary constraints should be offset with savings in other areas of the organization, since a strong and well-paid workforce is indispensable for success.

There are plenty of talented people in every organization who can be educated and trained to meet at least some of the needs for growth and new talent. Doing so has the added benefits of encouraging organizational loyalty and discouraging job burnout. Also, foresight can aid an organization in retraining and redeploying employees who might otherwise be adversely affected by a change in the organizational structure.

Customer satisfaction should be the primary goal of every employee. For some, this includes direct contact with patients; for others, the customer is an employee of this or some other partnering organization. All should be aware of who their customers are and take personal responsibility to be service-driven. Although this should be the goal of every health care organization, it is an unfortunate rarity within the health care world to find truly satisfied customers. Organizations that excel in this area stand out from the competition. Customer service training is the key to acquiring the skills necessary to correctly handle each and every situation that can arise. Praise, recognition, and rewards are effective methods of encouraging and sustaining high customer-service attributes.

Empowering employees to make suggestions and changes to the current way of doing business is an important and potentially very beneficial tool. Streamlining processes and looking for ways to eliminate cost and increase revenue are just two of the benefits of effective employee empowerment.

QUESTIONS TO PONDER

1. Has there been any recent attempt to discern employees' true motivational levels, as it regards their current job and your organization in general?

2. What are some ways that your organization can dramatically raise the general motivational level of the current employee base? How can they be communicated and implemented?

3. Does the current methodology for hiring employees encourage recruitment of outstanding employees? What does the first interview generally communicate about the organization?

4. Are potentially outstanding employees routinely turned away from the organization because there is no immediate perceived need for their skill sets? Why is this unwise?

5. Is employee turnover perceived as a problem for the organization? What is the competition offering that motivates people to leave? Are there other factors (job stagnation, lack of training opportunities, poor salary or benefits package, poor employee relations, poor community image, and so on) that contribute to the problem?

6. Do salary levels communicate the high value of the employees to the organization? Do employees sense that their jobs might be eliminated if profits are not sustained?

7. Is there any methodology in place that involves employees in a progressive education and training process in most departments of the organization?

8. Is there a strategic plan for retraining and redeploying employees who might be affected by potential changes within the dynamics or structure of the organization?

9. Are the majority of employees aware of a goal of high customer service?

10. Is employee empowerment at work within the organization at all? If not, why not?

CHAPTER 7

Purchasing

A Dynamic Model

Many a health care organization's purchasing procedures are archaic and need to be replaced rapidly to facilitate future long-term growth within the industry. Capital-equipment prices from manufacturers within the health care field are traditionally set on marketing models, as opposed to production-based pricing models. Therefore, health care organizations typically purchase major capital assets on the basis of a reduction from the manufacturer's list price. The health care industry seemingly stands alone in its use of this type of acquisition procedure, while other industries have taken extremely active roles in driving down pricing. Special attention needs to be paid not only to purchase of costly major capital equipment but also to the supply chain and distribution channels, which are also often loosely controlled and very wasteful.

The health care industry needs to look outside its own field to leaders in purchasing and distribution to fine tune these important procedures to better control cost and increase revenue. In addition, organizations need to tie purchasing models to strategic initiatives, comprehensively evaluate the total cost of new equipment purchases, and migrate closer to high-quality and cost-effective standardization within the industry. These important issues and many other related aspects are covered in depth in this chapter.

THE HEALTH CARE PURCHASING DILEMMA

Manufacturers and health care organizations share many common problems, costs, and barriers to sustained growth in the long run. Unfortunately, the manufacturing community has not equally shared the reductions in profitability and growth that have devastated the provider community. Reimbursement cuts and revenue losses have largely been borne by the provider community and only affected the manufacturing community in the form of delayed replacements, missed upgrades, and reduced option packages for new equipment.

The pendulum of cost cutting and major revenue losses is now about to swing toward the manufacturing and medical supply communities and will be evidenced by bankruptcy and reorganization, merger and acquisition, staff reduction, and major financial restructuring throughout this decade. Health care organizations have driven out every conceivable easily reduced cost and are now forced to look elsewhere for major reductions in operating costs. These reductions are most likely to come from the supply and equipment manufacturers who have ignored the need for equipment price concessions and have continued to sell equipment and supplies out of line with the research and development costs, production costs, and marketing costs of other technologically comparable industries.

Prices for major capital equipment and medical supplies within the health care industry are primarily based on marketing models and are usually not linked to the cost of production, research, and development or to return-on-investment (ROI) indexes commonly used by other industries.

Prices for major capital equipment and medical supplies within the health care industry are primarily based on marketing models and are usually not linked to the cost of production, research, and development or to return-on-investment (ROI) indexes commonly used by other industries. This high-cost method of price configuration and control represents extremely skewed pricing structures, which must be borne by the entire industry of health care providers.

A marketing-based pricing strategy uses industry list-price surveys to determine a range of prices in which a new product offering can be sold. This range of prices then sets the reduction from list-price that is used as a negotiation benchmark for the manufacturer's or vendor's sales staff. Pricing strategies based on market surveys are rarely representative of the actual cost of the product. Yet these artificial prices become the standard price from which all other industry-related costs are derived. For instance, salaries, bonuses, and other associated cost drivers are based on the revenues received from the sale of these products in the health care arena. Unfortunately, this practice has permeated the entire field of medicine. It is actually most comparable to the pricing strategies used by the entertainment and sports industries.

A production-based pricing strategy is a much more tightly controlled and cost-prohibitive setting; it is the common model in industries that are also quite technologically dependent (such as the automotive and aviation businesses). Production-based pricing strategies primarily add a predetermined ROI percentage to the total cost of production, which includes research and development, product placement, and marketing costs. Exhibit 7.1 demonstrates the major difference in product cost that can be easily traced to these two pricing strategies.

Pricing strategies based on market surveys are rarely representative of the actual cost of the product.

Unfortunately, market-pricing models are the norm for the entire health care industry. Artificial pricing is undoubtedly the biggest problem facing health care providers today. Everyone is looking to drive down costs during this era of decreasing reimbursement revenues. Individual hospitals

Exhibit 7.1. Market-Survey Versus Production-Cost Pricing Models

Ultrasound Machine (Production-Cost Pricing)

Cost of production	$39,000.00
Research and development (per unit cost)	12,000.00
Marketing and advertising	4,000.00
Total	55,000.00
Return on investment (ROI of 12%)	6,600.00
Minimum sale price	61,600.00

Ultrasound Machine (Market-Survey Cost Pricing)

Market leader top-end list-price survey	$312,000.00
Market leader low-end list-price survey	185,000.00
Trend-set leader survey—top end	295,000.00
Trend-set leader survey—low end	165,000.00
Market leader discount range	(10–22%)
Trend-set leader discount range	(15–24%)
List price for new ultrasound	305,000.00
Range of sale prices (same equipment)	231,800.00 to 274,500.00

and health systems will have trouble dramatically driving down sales prices without forming strategic alliances within the industry to combat this problem. Prices will not fall until industry leaders require accountability and proof of production cost from health care manufacturers.

IMPLEMENT FOR COMPARATIVE ANALYSIS

The key to long-term profitability and sustained growth for the industry is to look beyond the normal boundaries of health care for potential solutions to these important issues. Much of what needs to take place within health care happened in other industries years ago. I have already mentioned the near-collapse of the American automotive industry as a result of increased competition from Japanese automakers during the twenty-year period following 1970. The American manufacturers' survival required extensive industry retooling, reorganization, and creative leadership.

Chrysler stands out in people's memory as the most visible reminder of near death and revival. The manufacturer emerged from pending bankruptcy and a government bailout to become one of the most profitable automakers in recent history. The conversion was made possible because Chrysler committed itself to driving down costs wherever possible. After carving out costs from within, the company began forcing external suppliers to open their books so that costs of every component of the supply chain could be reduced. Vendors who would not comply with Chrysler's new way of business were quickly eliminated and replaced with other willing suppliers.

Equipment and supply costs must be realigned to match comparable technology and product costs from other industries.

This same approach must be taken within the entire health care industry. Equipment and supply costs must be realigned to match comparable technology and product costs from other industries. This process eliminates manufacturers' and suppliers' use of market-based pricing indexes and results in lower prices for every type of medical supply.

The importance of this reasoning can be demonstrated by comparing two similarly priced products that have contrasting levels of technology and pricing clearly not based on the cost of production. Suppose a hospital is considering replacement of a tray-line feeder for its cafeteria. The hospital obtains quotes from several vendors to replace the unit. Each vendor quotes the tray-line feeder at a replacement cost between $38,000 and $46,000. The unit is approximately twelve feet long and consists of a conveyor belt, an electrical motor, a drive gear, and several common drains. It is made of stainless steel and has a one-year warranty. Resale value of the unit after installation is probably less than 5 percent of the original cost of the unit.

Now compare the tray-line product with a comparably priced Lexus. The car has an engine, transmission, several microcomputers, an extensive electrical system, air conditioning, power steering, cruise control, air bags, leather seats, and a continuing list of such luxury features. Additionally, the Lexus comes with a five-year maintenance-free warranty and a strong resale value for years to come. As this simple example demonstrates, there is often no correlation between the cost of production and the market price.

ELEVATE PURCHASES TO A NEW PLANE

Many health care organizations treat the purchasing department as an extension of the financial and accounting office or some other normal, primary support service and do not extend any special training, hiring incentives, or bonus programs to its people. The lack of attention to this critical area of strategic potential means that the most talented and resourceful people in the purchasing field are not drawn to the medical industry. This translates into higher cost, sluggish growth, and wasted effort.

This process will not change until senior executives within the health industry view purchasing initiatives as strategic multipliers for growth. This needs to happen for two reasons. First, the health care industry relies heavily on technology to offer quality patient care and to drastically improve clinical outcomes. Second, the entire industry is critically dependent on medical supplies, pharmaceuticals, and other patient-treatment goods, which represent over 25 percent of total industry cost. The correlation of supply and equipment cost with future sustainable growth suggests that purchasing must be viewed as a strategic multiplier if health care providers are to remain competitive.

Further, the industry has already reached the point of highest possible return for the quick fixes used during the decade of the 1990s (for example, cutting staff, delaying purchases, and limiting training). Future sustainable growth will come from cost-cutting initiatives, which dramatically lower the acquisition cost of major capital equipment, revenue-producing expansions, and consumable supplies.

Currently, individuals with few negotiation skills (if any) typically bargain for price, term, and condition concessions. Likewise, purchase orders are frequently based on pricing and equipment configuration models orchestrated between the vendor and the physician or other primary-care provider, with no input from unbiased resources.

In contrast, quality purchase decisions stem from educated and well-trained staff who have been given the freedom to make long-range buying decisions founded on thorough research and a carefully orchestrated strategic buying plan or control methodology. Effective training, education, and compensation for key purchase personnel should be targeted at building programs and expertise that significantly limit the number of poor purchase decisions made within any fiscal period. Good purchase decisions prevent wasted dollars that are immediately attributable to the organization's bottom line. Here is a list of common mistakes made by purchasing personnel who have not been given the proper tools to become effective in a mission that is so important to any health care provider:

Common Purchasing Mistakes
- No systematic process for assessing the value of goods or services
- Reliance on in-house knowledge of pricing indexes, rebates, and competition offerings
- Historical purchasing trends not tracked or evaluated to aid in current purchases
- Repeat individual purchases not negotiated as a volume purchase amount
- Processes not streamlined enough to limit wasted effort, rework, and overstocks
- Restocking, freight, and returned goods fees not negotiated during purchase
- Installation charges not clearly defined
- Personnel not trained in negotiation skills

- Biased attraction present in purchasing decision (that is, personal preference)
- Competition not introduced adequately into the purchasing process
- Routine purchase of capital equipment based on piece-by-piece negotiations
- Payment terms not competitive with the industry
- Rebate and price-break opportunities not exercised within the allotted time
- Multiple purchases from the same vendor not captured as bulk purchasing
- Multiple purchases of like items not negotiated up front (for example, tires for a fleet)
- Product used in health care not compared to other industries (software, service costs)
- Source of supply not cost-effective for the volume of purchase
- Vendor or supplier cost not validated using common benchmarking methods
- Internet resources not used when appropriate
- Invoice procedures outdated and costly

LESSONS FROM WAL-MART

A dollar saved is much better than a dollar earned because earnings represent money that must be funneled through the hourglass of cost in order to determine the net revenue gained. Cost avoidance and dollars saved usually represent one-for-one returns to the bottom line because the gain is taken directly from the current cost of doing business. For instance, if the current number of patients seen in a health setting remains exactly the same but costs go down, then every dollar in cost savings represents a dollar of net revenue.

Sam Walton understood well this central truth and applied it to every conceivable application within the competitive retail industry. He proved to the world that a retail business could be successfully run with margins as small as 5–8 percent of total sales. If this is true for the highly volatile retail industry, then it stands to reason that it applies to the larger health care industry as well.

As an example of this truth in action, consider the savings potentially gained from strategically aligning capital-equipment purchases with the health care organization's long-term growth and financial-readiness goals. As a matter of practice, most health care organizations purchase capital equipment on a case-by-case basis whenever there is a perceived need for either ordinary replacement or improved patient treatment from a new product offering.

Quality purchase decisions stem from educated and well-trained staff who have been given the freedom to make long-range buying decisions founded on thorough research and a carefully orchestrated strategic buying plan or control methodology.

In a typical piece-by-piece negotiation process with the manufacturer, it is reasonable that a health care facility negotiate pricing incentives of 10–20 percent off normal list price. Much more can be gained if the institution carefully surveys every potential piece of capital equipment to be replaced in a three-to-five-year period and prenegotiates replacement of the equipment within the confines of a bundled purchase initiative or volume purchase agreement. The potential for savings or cost avoidance is significant. A preliminary assessment can be reached by analyzing the number and amount of capital-equipment purchases made within the preceding

Cost avoidance and dollars saved usually represent one-for-one returns to the bottom line because the gain is taken directly from the current cost of doing business.

> *Well-planned strategic capital acquisition purchases help prevent the erosion of profits often present when mistakes are made in hurried capital-equipment replacement.*

several years. This analysis can then be used to adequately predict the dollar amount of purchases likely to occur within the upcoming five years.

The organization can certainly realize additional savings of 10–15 percent or more by using such a method to prevent costly purchase of routinely replaced or upgraded capital equipment. This process should also extend to assessing new or discontinuing reimbursement procedures that affect revenue streams critical for future growth. Further, well-planned strategic capital acquisition purchases help prevent the erosion of profits often present when mistakes are made in hurried capital-equipment replacement. An institution can safely and easily negotiate a good deal if it is not pressured to meet these goals within a short time period.

USE ZERO-BASE PURCHASING

The safest way to ensure the best return on a purchase decision is to assume that all costs of purchase start with zero, until the manufacturer or vendor can quantifiably demonstrate value. This is especially true for the health care industry because of the wide use of pricing strategies based on market surveys. For instance, many surgical tools cost less than a hundred dollars to manufacture but carry price tags of hundreds and thousands of dollars when subsequently sold within the health care market.

Zero-base purchasing can be especially helpful with vendors who are selling highly intangible products (such as licensed software agreements) or those where it is difficult to assess the value. Vendors who are responsible for quantifying value often quickly concede their bottom price to get past the uncomfortable position of not knowing how to adequately talk about the cost of production or other comparisons of value.

In these cases, comparing similar software products from other industries may be the best way of getting a health care vendor to significantly concede on price issues. For instance, software use, fit, and functionality could be compared to Microsoft software products to force the vendor to relax claims of value when pricing indexes are severely skewed away from the more reasonably priced and widely available Microsoft products.

The value of zero-based purchasing can be further demonstrated by an example of nuclear medicine equipment purchase, as shown in Figure 7.1.

ELIMINATE BIASED ATTRACTIONS

Health care organizations often purchase equipment and supplies within a framework that allows individual bias toward a particular vendor or supplier. Biased attraction to vendor equipment can stem from a variety of sources, arising for instance during education and training of physicians

Figure 7.1. Purchase Price of Nuclear Camera with Coincidence Imaging and Attenuation Correction

and technical staff. Such bias often favors a particular vendor over another because personnel do not want to have to relearn techniques for treating patients (for example, another vendor's equipment may require new methods of operation). Although sometimes these issues and others like them are relevant, in many cases these biases are counterproductive to the organization's long-term goal of gaining the best overall value in acquiring new replacement equipment.

Biased attractions can usually be remedied by carefully controlling the approval process for major capital-equipment purchases.

Additionally, vendors often wine and dine personnel to secure a degree of ownership in the selection process. These biased attractions can usually be remedied by carefully controlling the approval process for major capital-equipment purchases. Physicians and other staff members should be consulted on the buying decision but not forced to compromise their position through purchase decisions that become rote because of physician or other staff buy-in prior to a legitimately negotiated purchase process.

Instead, physicians and other important staff members should be included as team members in the evaluation process. Their professional input is valuable and can prevent many mistakes in purchasing equipment that ends up not being acceptable to the community of health care providers who are responsible for sending patient populations to the various clinics, operating rooms, and other caregiving establishments. Here is a list of some critical evaluation and assessment issues that can be effectively reviewed by professional staffs to prevent poor purchasing decisions:

Professional Staff: Critical Links to Effective Purchasing Decisions

- Clinical outcomes from new and emerging technologies
- Impact on current operations (especially how business might change as a result of a purchase decision)
- Comparison to other community resources (indications of referral patterns)

- Risk-factor comparison and impact on patient discharge time line or cost

- Possible business disruption resulting from reimbursement dollars migrating from one group of practitioners to another (for instance, from radiologists to cardiologists)

EDUCATE BUYERS FOR LONG-TERM SUCCESS

Leading-edge technologies, resources, training, and best-practice initiatives should characterize purchasing departments. Personnel must be trained to streamline processes, negotiate cost-effective major purchases, and understand fully the total life-cycle cost of each and every critical supply. The additional training, equipment, and compensation costs to outfit these new departments are negligible when compared to the dollars currently wasted by untrained and ill-prepared health care organizations nationally.

As an example of this need to change current processes, consider the difference that training and proper research make in the purchase of the nuclear camera with coincidence imaging and attenuation correction shown in Figure 7.1. What is the probable range of savings that can be realized by an institution that employs a well-educated purchasing agent as opposed to an uneducated one? If we assume that the uneducated buyer would purchase the nuclear camera at the common discounted price (for example, 40 percent of market list price) and the educated buyer would purchase the camera at the best possible discounted price (say, 60 percent of market list price), then the difference paid is $260,000. This example represents only one purchase decision. Imagine the difference multiplied among hundreds of annual purchase decisions.

Now let's compare the cost of this mistake to the presumed high cost of specialized training to eliminate these problems. Usually training is not approved because there is no immediate quantifiable return on the investment for the institution. For instance, let's assume that the purchasing director has an opportunity to gain leading-edge training in the art of negotiation from a prestigious school such as Harvard University. A one-week training class costs $8,000, which includes tuition, travel, food, and

lodging. In all probability, most institutions would quickly deny the session, presuming it to be "excessive" and "unnecessary."

Now let's analyze the Harvard class to see if it meets the institution's assessment of "excessive" and "unnecessary." The class is offered as specialized training by the Harvard Graduate School of Business and is taught by one of the world's most respected names in negotiation. What is the probability that the purchasing director will not learn something of value during her one-week course, something that prepares her to better negotiate future hospital capital-equipment purchases? Chances are high that she will pick up incredible insights into the art of negotiation and drastically improve her current skill set.

This improvement would no doubt translate into significant future savings for the health care institution. In this case, Harvard University represents the institution that specializes in training, while the health care provider specializes in quality patient treatment. The best-practice initiatives for cost cutting are usually not found in service industries but rather in the teaching, training, and production industries.

RETAIN CONTROL IN THE BUYING DECISION

Technology can also be used to significantly lower the cost of capital acquisitions and other industry consumables. Purchasing departments rarely track the historical trends of purchasing decisions and thereby limit their ability to analyze and correct historical mistakes. For instance, computer programs can be used to track replacement trends, age and obsolescence issues, standardization opportunities, bulk purchase potential, freight and holding costs, and a multitude of similar cost-combative practices.

Purchasing departments rarely track the historical trends of purchasing decisions and thereby limit their ability to analyze and correct historical mistakes.

Streamlining Health Care Operations

Knowledge is indeed power if important decision-making criteria can be immediately accessed and used to render quality purchase decisions. For instance, one of the most common mistakes made in purchasing equipment and supplies is the tendency of purchasing personnel to rely solely on an immediate price concession as an incentive to do business with one vendor over another. As an example of the unreliability of this method, consider the furniture replacement scenario outlined in Table 7.1.

UNDERSTAND TOTAL PURCHASE COST

It is readily apparent from the analysis that the $95 chair represents the best long-term value for the organization. In this case, comparison of product

Table 7.1. Comparative Analysis of Furniture Vendors and Conversion to a Common Year Denominator

Comparative Analysis of Furniture Vendors

Item	Price	Replacement Time Frame	Warranty
Desk chair	$ 69	Three years	Ninety days
Desk chair	95	Five years	One year
Desk chair	125	Five years	One year

Conversion of Each Chair to a Common Year Denominator (That Is, Three and Five Converted to Fifteen)

Price	Quantity	Total Fifteen-Year Cost	Average Annual Cost
$ 69	25	$8,625 ($1,725 x 5)	$575
95	25	7,125 (2,375 x 3)	475
125	25	9,375 (3,125 x 3)	625

choices is fairly simple and can be assessed rather quickly. But many purchase decisions require lengthy analysis of total life-cycle cost to correctly determine the best fit and value for the organization.

In the case of capital-equipment replacements, the price of the equipment may be only a small portion of the total cost of purchase. Cath labs, CT scanners, and other major pieces of equipment may require extensive construction upgrade and retrofit costs, which can vary greatly from vendor to vendor. This is especially true when replacing a piece of equipment with another vendor's model. In some cases, installation and replacement costs can vary by hundreds of thousands of dollars for each project. Computer programs and modeling tools and software can help an institution prevent costly comparison mistakes and stretch each capital acquisition dollar to its maximum potential.

LINK DIRECTLY TO MANUFACTURERS

Many costs within the health care industry can be easily traced to the information gap between product manufacturers and the health care organizations they serve. Misconceptions about needs, patient-care delivery methods, and customer expectations translate into higher costs for production, research and development, marketing, distribution, and sales for both the manufacturer and the customer. Communication gaps between the manufacturer and the end user are even further complicated when other "middlepersons" seize the opportunity to create businesses that profit from this lack of information flow.

For instance, the health care industry boasts a wide assortment of professional agencies that negotiate national contract pricing agreements for their members. Unfortunately, many of these agencies have become so large and bureaucratic that they have ceased to deliver equitable cost savings for the marketplace. Additionally, these agencies negotiate standard discount rates for major capital equipment and other medical supplies without validating the cost of production or similar factors from the product manufacturer. These transaction sets then become arbitrary discount rates from list prices that the manufacturers have "predetermined." This type of negotiation standard does little to aid the industry in controlling long-term product cost.

This practice has created a false ceiling of pricing, which hides many other high-cost variables such as rebate incentives that flow back to the contract agencies. These rebates represent costs, which are in addition to the annual membership costs solicited from the member health care organization. The costs are often camouflaged as administrative fees, volume purchase incentives, and other similar practices that end up costing the health care industry billions of dollars annually.

Purchasing agencies negotiate standard discount rates for major capital equipment and other medical supplies without validating the cost of production or similar factors from the product manufacturer.

The negotiating tactics of large corporations can be used effectively if they are tied to investigative processes. Manufacturers are much more likely to open their books and share production cost information if required to do so as a prerequisite to negotiation for a major national contract, especially if the practice becomes common throughout the entire industry (again, as with the automotive and aviation industries).

Although some aspects of the negotiation process can still be handled by group purchasing agencies, there is a large gap in the flow of information between manufacturers and end users that needs to be closed

Manufacturers and health care organizations need to develop relationships within the industry that promote methods for lowering the overall total cost of industry products.

if unnecessary product costs are to be eliminated. Manufacturers and health care organizations need to develop relationships within the industry that promote methods for lowering the overall total cost of industry products to include the cost of training, repairs, supply parts, technical interfaces, and so forth. Virtually every segment of the health care industry contains pricing structures, which are completely out of line with comparable technology costs in other industries. Here are some additional areas that should be improved in the critical link between manufacturers and health care organizations:

- Facilities and equipment placement planning
- Equipment interface requirements and opportunities
- Multifocused training (that is, for providers, technicians, and service personnel)
- Technology trends and potential patient-care impact
- Research efforts that focus on provider-to-patient real-time interaction

CONSIDER NEW AND EMERGING DISTRIBUTION MODELS

The health care industry relies heavily on supply distribution processes, which are archaic and costly. These costs are driven by several factors: extensive reliance on overnight product deliveries, multiple warehousing layers, subsequent inventory handoffs, and so on. Participants in the health care industry for the most part do not track inventory holding costs, transportation and delivery costs, or similar supply distribution variables to the degree that other competitive industries do. This relaxed atmosphere of control in the cost of equipment and supply distribution has permeated the entire industry and is stealing valuable reimbursement revenue from the provider communities. Refer to Figure 7.2 for a comparison of the layers of warehousing common to the health care market.

Good distribution processes are carefully controlled and redundancies eliminated in each subprocess. There are many variables to supply distribution, which should be improved within the industry to better align health

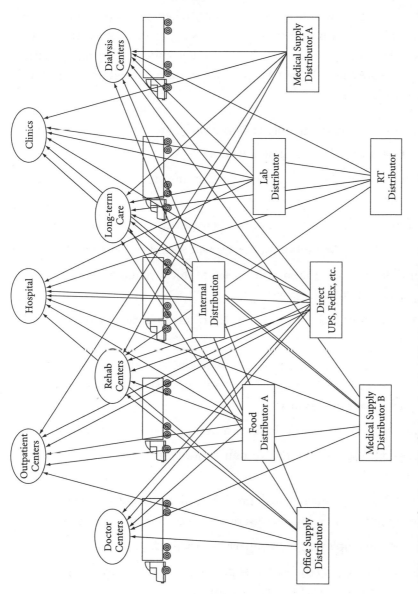

Figure 7.2. Distribution Attributes in Health Care Industry

Source: Provided by Joe Smith, president, National Health Care Logistics (NHCL). Used with permission. 570 Grand Dr., Cleveland, TN 37312.

care with best-practice results from other industries (such as distribution models from Wal-Mart or Publix). Best-practice initiatives include methodology for measuring optimum reorder quantity, better transportation space utilization, extensive automation and tracking mechanisms, and other methods for constantly reducing the cost of equipment and supply distribution. Here are some of the best-practice initiatives used by the market leaders in other industries:

Methods for Controlling Supply Distribution Cost

- Create strategies for reducing inventory.
- Eliminate waste through computer and communications tracking technology.
- Automate warehouse procedures to maximize inventory turnover.
- Study and improve motion, space, transport, and personnel utilization.
- Schedule processes that minimize safety stock, economic order quantity, and lead ordering time.
- Maximize fleet usage from every distribution partner (internal and external).
- Expand warehousing hours to eliminate idle equipment and other factors of waste found in normal shift operation (twenty-four-hour versus eight-hour operations).
- Consolidate distribution channels among all common suppliers.
- Track daily usage of product from manufacturer to end user (real-time data).
- Use forecasting models, which predict usage from historical trends and similar data (that is, logic software and other software applications).
- Cross-train employees to be multitask-oriented.
- Use third-party warehouses, equipment, and personnel to lower total overall industry costs for every participant.

The health care industry needs to address these wasteful supply and equipment distribution problems and support efforts within the industry to change archaic practices. Efforts to break away from existing costly enterprises serve to wake up the industry to much-needed changes. Companies such as National Health Care Logistics (NHCL) are striving to cut through these barriers to change and create options by which a health care organization can reduce the costs of supply distribution. These organizations face many obstacles along the path to a better future for the health care industry. Resistance to change resembles what the formidable retail industry experienced as Sam Walton set out to change things. Hopefully, today's health care "pioneers for change" will be just as successful in eliminating needless waste.

TRACK TRANSPORTATION-RELATED COST

Transportation costs consume 5–10 percent of the total cost of supplies and equipment delivered throughout the health care industry. This is definitely a category of cost that must be carefully examined, measured, and controlled to further the revenue-protection goals of the industry.

Manufacturers of medical products frequently do not use cost-effective methods for meeting customer requests. For instance, the health care industry uses a disproportionate amount of overnight delivery to support daily business operations. This cost often directly correlates to inconsistency in product delivery to health care organizations. In other words, providers react to normally poor delivery methods by overemphasizing reliable though costly overnight delivery. In many cases, shoddy delivery practices are caused by poor inventory and production control and then passed on to the health care provider community in the form of higher product prices and expensive transportation costs. This will not change until these events are adequately investigated and remedied.

The blame for high transportation costs does not rest solely on the

Shoddy delivery practices are caused by poor inventory and production control and then passed on to the health care provider community in the form of higher product prices and expensive transportation costs.

manufacturing community. Health care organizations, as well, often make arbitrary decisions about the best transportation option to use. In many cases, overnight delivery and other high-cost transportation solutions (such as those in the next list) are really not necessary when analyzed against issues such as the criticality of need, on-hand quantity, due-in quantity, physician or provider preference (not need), and other decision criteria.

Inefficiency in Transport and Delivery
- Reliance on supplier or manufacturer shipping price indexes
- Cargo capacity not used to maximize cubic volume, weight, or height
- Routing and shipping destination and return points not coordinated efficiently
- Terms of delivery not specified adequately to prevent damage or waste
- Freight forwarding services not used when appropriate
- Safety stocks and reorder points inappropriate for volume of business
- Due-in and on-hand quantities as well as product substitution choices not analyzed correctly
- Issues and receipts not bar-coded for fast replenishment and tracking
- Outdated procedures, untrained staff, and unnecessary rework
- Transportation-related costs not trended or captured as reference for cost reduction
- Last-minute high-cost orders (overnights) not tracked for causal relationship
- Vendors and suppliers not charged back for delay, inefficiency, and damaged goods
- No one tasked with the responsibility to track transportation-related costs or similar delivery issues
- No cross-docking (truck-to-truck) operations or other efficient methods of product delivery and control

Unnecessary transportation-related costs are also linked to hauling capacity. Optimum shipping size, weight, and cargo configuration constraints are controlled within the health care industry much less than in other industries. For example, trucks bound for Wal-Mart stores are filled to capacity and routed using sophisticated computer software so that every dollar of transportation-related cost is maximized for its highest possible return. This includes prenegotiation for fueling, repairs, services, scheduled stops, and back-haul capacity (that is, returned items coming back to the distribution center).

ELIMINATE RETURNS, DAMAGED GOODS, AND LIABILITY

Many health care manufacturers and suppliers commonly charge 20–50 percent of the purchase price as a restocking fee when customers return merchandise. It is unfortunate that a high-cost return policy is rarely factored into the prepurchase decision since many of these policies and practices can be eliminated or drastically reduced when negotiated up front in the purchase process. This is especially critical if suppliers help quantify the amount of supplies needed. It is often the case for a new account that the manufacturer's representative works with the health care provider to establish initial order amounts.

Damaged goods can be a costly commodity as well, especially with manufacturers who practice haphazard or careless handling procedures. These costs are often passed onto the medical community because boxes and other containers are not always opened or examined for several days or weeks after delivery. The typical

Well-trained employees can prevent waste and spot careless handling by vendors and suppliers.

health care organization can be characterized by careless handling procedures as well. Untrained or uncaring employees can be costly to an organization. On the other hand, well-trained employees can prevent waste and spot careless handling by vendors and suppliers. These issues should be corrected immediately and tracked to protect against future waste.

Liability for damaged or spoiled goods can essentially be eliminated by installing proactive shipping and receiving procedures. Organizations often get into trouble because they attempt to cut staff to a minimum level, which makes problem prevention nearly impossible. These mistakes can be avoided by carefully tracking both the degree of occurrence and the quantity and cost of damaged, returned, lost, or incorrectly shipped goods.

INSTALL PROACTIVE PAYMENT PROCEDURES

The health care industry routinely pays bills sixty to ninety days after receipt. This practice is costly for both the supplier and the health care provider. Many organizations ignore prepay, early-pay, and other discount incentives because staff are often too busy to pick up on these cost-saving opportunities. Additionally, health care organizations often claim that third-party payer reimbursements are too slow to allow them to pay receipts faster than the revenue stream flow. This is definitely a problem for the entire industry, but there are workable solutions available to prevent losing incentive dollars for proactive payment. For instance, receipts can be organized by early-pay incentive, late-payment cost, and similar strategies to reflect the most efficient method of maximizing the value of available cash.

Closely related to this issue is payment of penalties or late fees for overdue accounts and other cost structures. Accounting personnel often pay receipts on a first-in, first-out (FIFO) basis regardless of the structure of the bill or invoice. This area of payment procedure should also be realigned to maximize the cash preservation benefit. Additionally, proactive accounting personnel who are trained to call these companies and request early-pay discounts can win hidden discounts or incentives. This is especially true for larger invoices.

SUMMARY

Health care organizations have borne the burden of reducing costs in the health care field; they need to pass on these cost reductions to manufacturers, who have been virtually unaffected by the recent cuts. Although health care organizations have shaved staff and procedures way back, vendors and manufacturers have continued to profit on their highly priced equipment and supplies. These primarily market-based pricing policies have little to do with the streamlined pricing structure found in other industries. Savvy health care organization managers have to find new ways to obtain pricing pegged more closely to a production-based pricing strategy. Those that succeed will undoubtedly save their organizations countless dollars in the annual equipment budget.

It is important for health care organizations to look upon the purchasing process as a strategic multiplier for sustained growth. This is rarely the case now, with important purchasing, term, and condition decisions being assigned to lower-level managers or clerks who are inadequately trained to analyze the strategic purchasing processes within their organization. This is unwise given that capital purchases, medical supplies, pharmaceuticals, and other goods represent a tremendous portion of any budget.

Innovative purchasing practices, rarely found in the health care world but available for analysis from other industries, are an important benchmark for health care. Such ideas as negotiated bundled purchases, aligning capital-equipment purchases with the organization's long-term growth and financial-readiness goals, and using zero-base purchasing to analyze manufacturers are ways to move toward purchasing efficiency.

Eliminating unnecessarily biased preference toward a vendor or manufacturer is a key method for increasing purchasing effectiveness. Additionally, proper training of buyer groups is imperative to success, especially in such highly technical decision-making processes. Examining the true benefit of using professional buying agencies rather than negotiating directly with manufacturers is called for.

Likewise, the supply distribution and transportation processes currently in place in health care are highly inefficient and costly. There are several distribution models available that demonstrate how efficiently distribution and transportation processes can be. Health care organizations would be wise to adopt many of these logistically superior processes.

Other areas of concern include examining restocking fees; damaged goods policy; and liability responsibility for damaged, unnecessary, or spoiled goods. The various costs involved in these procedures often penalize the health care organization greatly; they can be reduced through proper management and prenegotiated agreement. Along the same lines, is the often overlooked advantage of early and proactive payment procedures. Incentives for early payment, as well as eliminating late fees, save an organization additional money.

QUESTIONS TO PONDER

1. Is your organization comparing purchasing practices to other health care entities or best-practice initiatives from other industries?

2. How many normal purchases wouldn't appear so normal if viewed in light of the Lexus versus tray-line feeder example?

3. Are the logistics associated with the health care industry really that different from what is present in the retail, automotive, and aviation industries? If not, why is there such a great cost difference?

4. Do streamlined organizational charts always translate into less cost?

5. What percentage of your annual budget goes to training? Does this represent cost, or cost avoidance?

6. How well is your organization tracking historical cost or purchase trends? What can be done to make it better?

7. Are contract prices for capital equipment and medical supplies being negotiated competitively within the health care industry?

8. How many layers of warehousing and inventory handoffs exist between you and the manufacturers of medical products?

9. Is someone in your organization tracking transportation-related costs?

10. What percentage of annual purchases are wasted through returned or damaged goods?

11. Are invoice payment procedures proactive enough to maximize the value of short-term cash?

12. How well would your organization rate in meeting the objectives of the dynamic purchasing model described in this chapter?

CHAPTER 8

Strategic Technology Assessment

Not Just an Acquisition

Technology assessment is becoming strategically necessary for any health care organization that hopes to remain effective and financially viable. This field involves careful analysis of capital acquisitions, including product price and life-cycle issues, demographic and utilization studies, and other strategically based analyses. Organizations that neglect this important function suffer from the critical inefficiencies inherent in poor equipment planning and the costly mistakes associated with expensive and unnecessary purchases.

Technology assessment should be a strategic driver to business performance. The component pieces that make this possible are objective economic evaluation, market acquisition factors, standardization methodologies, life-cycle value analysis, reliability and repair issues, committee involvement, and others. This chapter addresses these strategic components of technology assessment and shows your organization how to use these critical functions to leapfrog ahead and improve both market position and patient-provider satisfaction.

A CRITICAL STEP IN COST AVOIDANCE

Technology assessment is a critical process that requires an institution to strategically align purchases with long-term goals. This alignment process should include budget review, clinical needs, emerging and existing health care treatment standards, local physician referral patterns, and the strategic business development goals of the health care organization. Poor technology assessment processes lead to unnecessary major capital acquisition, improperly aligned patient treatment plans, and unpredictable paths of patient referral from physicians. Worse, each of these areas of poor technology planning leads to higher patient delivery costs and lost revenue.

Technology planning affects the revenue stream and patient treatment costs in a variety of ways. In recent years, many health care organizations have postponed new equipment purchases to cut annual operating expenses. This practice can backfire significantly if not correctly administered. For instance, delays in purchasing capital equipment may actually erode current business if the new technology represents the normal standard, or the best standard, of patient treatment. Likewise, purchase delays often prevent or constrain an organization from capturing new market business and allow competitors to reach a new market first.

Delays in purchasing capital equipment may actually erode current business if the new technology represents the normal standard, or the best standard, of patient treatment.

Inappropriate purchases of new technology can be extremely wasteful, especially if capital equipment or upgrades are purchased without regard to the strategic goals of the organization. Physicians and other primary caregivers regularly request equipment for procedures and patient treatment standards that are declining or nonreimbursable. These purchases must be closely examined since patient-treatment methodologies usually change quickly under this sort of circumstance. Additionally, a treatment path might represent a trial treatment avenue, which may become obsolete after a short period of time. This is especially true of emerging procedures that do not yet have FDA approval. Purchase success in these areas requires much more due diligence in the preassessment phase to adequately predict the likelihood of industrywide acceptance of the emerging treatment procedures and standards. Here are some common technology assessment program goals:

- Improve the quality of patient care
- Reduce annual operating costs
- Increase physician and provider referrals
- Align acquisitions with market goals
- Decrease patient wait and stay periods
- Maximize reimbursement revenues
- Create a market niche; stimulate growth
- Reduce operator error and litigation cases

In technology purchasing, new may not always be better. Sometimes technologies remain virtually unchanged for years before a major breakthrough changes the underlying basic clinical use. Manufacturers often repackage the same technology to appear significantly improved when in fact no real change has taken place within the field. In such an instance, a new equipment purchase is often of little value from the point of view of health care delivery. This is why it is so important for an organization to have a proactive technology assessment program in place, including input from a variety of subject matter experts.

Manufacturers often repackage the same technology to appear significantly improved when in fact no real change has taken place within the field.

CREATE AN OBJECTIVE ECONOMIC EVALUATION MODEL

Technology has a heavy impact on the quality and cost of patient treatment within the health care industry. A new technology may appear extremely costly when viewed as a major capital acquisition but actually lower the cost of treatment substantially once other important economic factors are added to the evaluation equation (such as a decrease in the number of patient stay days, increased treatment capacity as a result of improved patient through-put, and lower litigation costs). New technologies also open or close avenues of reimbursement and may cause treatment procedures to migrate from one group of practitioners to another. Each element of potential change must be looked at as an integral part of the economic evaluation model of the strategic technology assessment process. Here are some of the impor-tant decision factors present in this assessment:

Technology Assessment Economic Evaluation Factors
- Reimbursement trends
- Current or potential physician referral patterns
- Market penetration, regional or national acceptance and use
- Patient outcomes, quality of care, and customer acceptance
- FDA approval or likelihood of approval
- Migration of treatment base (from one group of physicians to another)
- Staffing changes to include training and availability of support per-sonnel
- Patient and provider safety or risk issues
- Support for technology to include facility upgrades, network issues, and utility costs
- Relationship to long-term strategic and operational goals

An economic evaluation of technology must also include thorough assessment of the treatment populations of both the existing patient base and the expected demographic changes of the emerging patient population. This prevents problems of overpurchase and underpurchase related to the technology acquisition process. Health care organizations often fail to cor-rectly predict how long it takes to build an adequate patient referral base. This is especially true for new technologies and procedures. Patient refer-ral patterns are also greatly affected by the time that has passed since the

Streamlining Health Care Operations

new technology or procedure was developed. A market that has delayed implementation of industry-accepted practice for a long period of time will probably reach full referral potential much more quickly than one where a new and emerging procedure is implemented immediately.

This relationship between technology or procedure availability and the time taken to implement is very important because technology emplacements are most effective and show the highest possible return on investment when linked to the growth patterns of the referral network. For instance, a hospital that is considering purchasing an expensive stand-alone PET (positron emission tomography) device might find that it is best served by first installing a new nuclear camera with coincidence imaging and attenuation correction. The resulting patient base from the new nuclear camera could then be used to support subsequent acquisition of a much more costly PET system.

> *Technology emplacements are most effective and show the highest possible return on investment when linked to the growth patterns of the referral network.*

MAKE MARKET-DRIVEN PURCHASES

There are many factors in the technology assessment review process that should be defined by prevailing market conditions. A strategic assessment of fit and use must include thorough analysis of the payback period of the investment, the highest and best use of capital acquisition dollars, and the expected rate of return. Closely related to this are demographic studies of the patient population, including payer mix, discharge expense rates (prepurchase and postpurchase comparison), the relationship between inpatient and outpatient procedures, and the potential dollar effects that changes in current procedures would make in existing billing or cost structures.

Utilization rates should also be factored into the assessment process of market-based technology acquisition. This is especially true given the recent changes in how the Health Care Financing Administration (HCFA) and Medicare are setting reimbursement rates for the industry. New rate schedules are generally tied to the current or expected volume of procedures to be handled nationally. In many of these cases, identical clinical treatment procedures receive totally different reimbursement rates even though the cost of the equipment acquisition remains the same.

Technology assessment should also be used for a product upgrade as well. An upgrade or enhancement can be very costly and should be analyzed for its market-related potential. Further, manufacturers often push low-end equipment for initial placement into health care organizations with the intention of selling upgrades and option packages to the user at a later date. This type of practice is usually very costly to the health care entity and frequently represents hidden cost because the so-called options end up being required items once the community of primary caregivers realizes that the technology is available. These practices are likewise difficult to undo because options for obtaining the technology elsewhere (from another vendor) often require the health care organization to repurchase the same level of original equipment.

Option packages and other upgrade paths are usually more expensive to purchase for an installed piece of equipment than for a brand new one. Additionally, the health care organization usually enjoys the most leveraged buying and negotiation power during the initial purchase period. The manufacturer often has a distinct advantage in selling upgrades in the postpurchase arena because upgrades and options may be available only from the primary vendor. This problem is similar to what new car buyers experience when they want to add an additional feature to a car after it has been delivered from the factory. The dealer-installed price for the same basic feature is usually much higher than the manufacturer's price. Worse yet is the cost of features that are installed after delivery of the car (that is, not during the purchase at the dealer), which tends to be even higher. Here are some additional standards to be considered when analyzing technologies for future acquisition:

Market Acquisition Factors

- How soon does the technology need to be in place to meet acquisition goals?
- What is the reliability of existing equipment?
- Will the equipment be used to its maximum capacity? If not, what is the minimum acceptable level of utilization to meet return-on-investment goals?
- What patient-treatment changes will occur as a result of the purchase? Will these changes affect the standard of care within the health care organization?
- Does this acquisition create reimbursement changes for other caregiving practices?
- Can the equipment being replaced be used somewhere else (say, in a physician group practice)?
- Is equipment compatible with related systems, such as Digital Imaging and Communications in Medicine (DICOM) standards, Local Area Network (LAN) standards, and so on?
- Can equipment be supported using current maintenance personnel or service-related practices?
- Have marketing issues been addressed in the acquisition plan to maximize the potential of physician referral?

STANDARDIZE ACQUISITION PRACTICES

The health care industry is moving more and more toward standardized practices. Standardization goals are good if the product or practice being standardized is of high quality and clearly demonstrates value to the customer (that is, the patient or the provider community). In the technology assessment arena, standardization practices can translate into large savings because variable costs can often be reduced or eliminated (training, supplies, parts, repair rates, installation charges, utility rates, and so on, all of which affect the overall life-cycle cost of a product). Standardizing can significantly reduce many of these variable costs because the presence of multiple vendors usually represents fragmented pricing structures and subsequent higher costs.

The initial acquisition price is often only a small portion of the total life-cycle cost of a product. In many cases, the highest initial product cost may actually have a much lower life-cycle cost. This is so with manufacturers who consistently build equipment with high reliability and quality control standards. Strict production control methods often translate into lower equipment repair rates, less down time, and fewer subcomponent replacements. Likewise, some product manufacturers purposely price their products much lower for entry to offset the customer's investigation into product reliability and related long-term ownership cost.

Standardization also benefits an organization from the perspective of training and interoperability. Like equipment and technology usually results in less operator train-up time, creates more cross-functional utilization, and increases patient throughput. This is especially true if the technology is of high quality and represents best-practice use within the industry. A number of critical standardization issues should be considered when implementing a technology assessment program:

Product quality	Repair history
Ease of use	Safety issues
Performance	Initial price
Supply costs	Warranty
Preferences	Utility cost
Connectivity	Contract rates
Utilization	Marketability
Inventory	Disposal value
Upgrade path	Clinical use
Flexibility	Installation costs

DO A TOTAL LIFE-CYCLE ANALYSIS

The initial acquisition cost of capital equipment usually represents only a small portion of the total cost of ownership. In many cases, the postpurchase cost varies significantly from one equipment manufacturer to another. Cost varies because manufacturers exercise a variety of quality control methodologies in their research and development, subcomponent supply chain, and production processes. As an example of this, consider how product quality is affected by such common production decisions as the percentage of acceptable defects allowed in a shipment of circuit boards from a subcontractor. One manufacturer may accept a 5 percent defect rate, while another accepts as high a rate as 10 percent. Worse yet are the manufacturers that do not validate quality control issues until the postproduction process (that is, check machines as they are ready to leave the factory).

In the previous example, it is readily apparent that simple manufacturing decisions such as this can create a much greater postpurchase cost. Equipment reliability affects the costs of subsequent maintenance and service, which tend to grow over time. Unreliable equipment manifests itself in lower overall utilization rates, lost procedural revenues, and dissatisfied user-provider relationships. These in turn can lead to changing physician referral patterns and lost market opportunity. In many cases, these problems go unnoticed and uncorrected, thus producing negative effects with uncertain root causes. Here are some common maintenance and service-related costs, which can vary greatly from one vendor or manufacturer to another:

- Hourly, after-hour, and holiday service repair rates
- Service manuals and special tools needed to repair equipment
- Cost of service training for biomedical or clinical engineering staff
- Special software license agreements
- Manufacturer's ability to conduct remote access diagnostic repair and analysis

- Discount rate on repair parts and supplies

- Annual service agreement cost

- Extent and type of warranty coverage

- Equipment up-time guarantee and reimbursement

- Availability of alternative resources for repair parts or service

Equipment-related supply expenses are often the most costly issues associated with capital acquisition. Unfortunately, these costs are not always considered as part of the initial purchase evaluation criteria. Lab equipment replacements are a common example of this problem. Chemical reagent and other supply costs usually represent 90 percent or more of the cost of running lab tests. This is true because many of these tests are run automatically by machines, with very little input from the personnel working in the lab (aside from loading test tubes and turning on the machine). Reagent cost tends to be erratic and can account for major differences in individual test costs. This is especially true for manufacturers who promote sole use of their reagent with the installed machine.

In many cases, these problems are further complicated because the organization has limited available capital dollars, to the point that personnel become creative in getting new equipment. For instance, lab personnel may receive new equipment for free just by signing a five-year exclusive chemical reagent agreement. In many instances, these agreements are signed without evaluating the reagent cost against standards in other industries. The reagent agreement usually represents an operating budget issue that does not require board or similar approval. Even in instances where higher approval is needed, these purchases often appear to be required in order to transact daily business.

Type of financing, construction and structural alteration costs, training and applications issues, accreditation standards, disposal and removal costs, and so on also affect total life-cycle costs. Each area must be reviewed independently and collectively to determine the overall impact and quality of the prospective manufacturer or vendor's offering. The next checklist outlines many of the critical issues that need to be examined to understand the total life-cycle cost of equipment. Technology assessment teams should be formed to evaluate these functions adequately to prevent unnecessary costs and poor purchase decisions.

Sample Life-Cycle Assessment Checklist

☐ Is the vendor price-competitive with the industry? Does the assessment include all options and related postpurchase costs?

☐ What installation, interface, or connectivity issues should be included?

☐ Are architectural drawings and other design and review costs included in the analysis?

☐ What construction or structural change costs are required to operate the equipment?

☐ Has a qualified attorney reviewed the purchase contract or maintenance agreement to determine hidden costs?

☐ What is the annual expected utility cost?

☐ Have reimbursement issues been considered?

☐ Does this purchase create a need to recruit, hire, train, or dismiss personnel?

☐ Have maintenance, service, and repair issues been analyzed for future cost?

☐ What are the costs associated with evaluating the technology (consulting fees, staff review time, vendor negotiation expense)?

☐ Has a thorough financial evaluation been conducted, including leasing cost, lending fees, present or future dollar value analysis, and similar costs?

☐ Are there marketing issues that need to be considered as part of the total cost?

☐ Have disposal or environmental-related costs been included in the analysis?

☐ Are there any discount rates available in the product offering (for example, payment terms, future part or service discounts, additional purchase incentives)?

USE REVIEW COMMITTEES EFFECTIVELY

A range of complicated technology is used throughout the health care industry; no individual is going to have the expertise needed to correctly evaluate all of the possible acquisitions. Therefore, the organization must set up an effective evaluation committee or committees that pool knowledge and experience from the multiple disciplines represented by the modalities and specialized areas related to the technology. The process for evaluating each technology should be controlled and orchestrated by an individual or team, using methods and procedures that can be applied systematically to each evaluation.

Most of the issues surrounding technology review and comparison study can be quantified, measured, and evaluated comprehensively enough to eliminate any personal bias, vendor preference, or similar distraction that might otherwise negatively influence the decision-making process. When handled correctly, technology assessment review can be used to align purchases with the long-term goals and initiatives of the health care organization. This in turn maximizes the ROI potential for each major capital acquisition.

The technology-review process usually requires committee members to understand not only the technology itself but also how its use affects day-to-day operation of the entire health care provider continuum. For instance, procedural use of a new technology may involve a change in use of surgical supplies, treatment processes, the level of patient or provider risk, and other events that greatly affect the overall cost and quality of the acquisition itself.

Committee members should be assigned responsibility for gathering critical information related to the proposed study. In many cases, this information-gathering process includes review of the current literature, available research material, telephone and personal interviews with subject matter experts, and historical data from the vendor or manufacturer and the user community. This next list identifies common areas for research to support a committee technology-review process:

Avenues for Committee Technology Research

Biomedical staff	Physician and nursing
Technical users	IS and IT personnel
Pharmacy and materials	Purchasing staff
Vendor community	Manufacturers
Research groups	Articles and studies
Food and Drug Administration	Accreditation body
Legal and risk staff	Related industries
Financial staff	Other users

A good way to keep a technology-review committee moving along effectively is to ensure that each study has a predetermined charter or a range of objectives that reflect the needs of the health care organization. For instance, a committee might be given a mission to decide whether to purchase a replacement angio suite for an older existing system. The charter might include a requirement to review all possible solutions, from replacing the system to analyzing whether a multipurpose room or similar replacement device could handle the current and future patient volumes. Additionally, the committee might be asked to look at utilization rates from the entire provider community to determine if a tighter patient-scheduling model can be created to move existing patients from one facility to another and avoid purchasing a new replacement unit. Here is a list of ten key factors that should be considered when establishing or chartering a new review committee:

Committee Charter Essentials

1. Define the scope and nature of the review project.
2. Validate the need for the technology so as to prevent unnecessary purchase.
3. Eliminate any biased attraction in the review process.

4. Hold each member responsible for educating the group on his or her research activity.

5. Define all review process time frames and target decision dates.

6. Evaluate all research data for accuracy, quality, and completeness.

7. Create a process that involves everyone in decision making.

8. Emphasize the relationship of the review to the established goals of the organization.

9. Fix responsibility for separate performance review functions.

10. Effectively communicate the findings of the committee to the entire organization.

A review committee is an integral part of a successful technology assessment process. Its overall success depends on personnel understanding the importance of maintaining a cross-functional relationship and an open-minded research mentality. A number of factors can limit the effectiveness of the review process if not handled correctly. For instance, many providers have vested years of training in particular patient-treatment procedures and may be understandably opposed to adopting equipment or a methodology that alters their treatment of patients. This is often true even when research clearly shows that one particular treatment may be more or less effective than another. Good communication and negotiation skills are necessary ingredients in sidestepping such problems. Additionally, providers and staff may be accustomed to a particular vendor's equipment and resist efforts to adequately evaluate alternative choices. In many cases, involving the parties in the evaluation process and carefully linking each decision point to a clinically and quantifiably based research process can help solve any problems.

SUMMARY

Technology assessment is a growing field within the health care world, one that can greatly affect the revenue stream and patient-treatment costs in a variety of ways. Both postponement of purchase and inappropriate purchase can adversely affect the efficiency of an organization. These mistakes are widespread, however, and reflect an industry that often does not include technology assessment as a key component in strategic planning.

Also, it is imperative that a strategic analysis be maintained to ensure the payback period of investment, the highest and best use of capital acquisition dollars, and the expected rate of return. Demographic and utilization studies should be included in the technology assessment process.

Technology assessment goes beyond the bounds of simply purchasing capital equipment; it should be applied in negotiating product upgrades, supplies, warranties, and service. This allows the health care organization the most leverage and eliminates the need to continuously reanalyze a purchase during its entire life cycle.

Standardization in technology assessment should not imply lower quality but instead streamlining of an inefficient methodology for capital-equipment acquisition. This is primarily true in regard to the variable costs associated with capital acquisitions: training, supplies, parts, repair rate, installation charge, utility rate, and so on.

Technology assessment can also serve as a means for analyzing the total life cycle of equipment. This is important because initial price is only a fraction of the total cost of the product. Other component costs (repair, supply, utilization, disposal, lost revenue, dissatisfaction of users and providers) are key issues of importance to the entire life cycle.

During the life-cycle analysis and in the strategic review of technology assessment, it is important to use committees to effectively evaluate proposed acquisitions. Key persons within an organization can pool knowledge and experience from the multiple disciplines represented by the modalities and specialized areas of expertise.

QUESTIONS TO PONDER

1. Is the technology assessment process strategically aligned with the long-term goals of the organization?

2. Are there areas of declining physician referral that might reflect eroded or lost business caused by delayed, missed, or inappropriate capital-equipment acquisition?

3. How frequently is equipment replaced on account of age, without looking into the degree of current utilization or technological obsolescence?

4. Does your organization's capital-acquisition process include extensive evaluation of contributing economic factors?

5. What percentage of equipment upgrades to existing purchased equipment occur within two years of initial purchase? Would these options be purchased more economically during the initial period?

6. Is capital equipment being put into use without going through a review process? If so, are any of these emplacements tied to using medical supply agreements or similar secondary arrangements?

7. Does your organization follow a process for determining the total life-cycle cost of equipment and supplies?

8. What standardization practices are common to the organization? Are efforts to reduce supplier variability encouraged or discouraged?

9. How important is the initial equipment price to the overall vendor selection process? Are purchase decisions more reflective of initial price than of overall quality?

10. Are equipment reliability standards a major consideration in purchase decisions?

CHAPTER 9

Utilization Management Within Technology Assessment

S ubstantial major equipment purchasing dollars are completely wasted by health care organizations because of a lack of proper needs analysis. Replacement equipment is often purchased without looking at the history or percentage of daily use, reimbursement or funding changes, or other conditions. Some organizations purchase additional equipment, such as imaging labs and other high-dollar capital equipment, unnecessarily when patient volume could easily be absorbed through better patient and physician scheduling models or other purchase-avoidance techniques.

Many mistakes of this sort can be eliminated through strong utilization research and management. With the high cost of medical equipment, it is certainly an area that deserves vigilance and fine-tuning. Aside from the initial cost of equipment, utilization studies assess ongoing and future use, idle time, and continuous evaluation of market changes.

This chapter addresses the need to incorporate a thorough utilization management program into every health care organization and demonstrates the benefits associated with the efforts taken in this area. Although utilization management is often considered a subset of technology assessment, it is critical to cost avoidance and revenue preservation and therefore addressed, in this chapter, as a distinct topic.

Other closely related topics in this chapter are process reengineering as a purchase-avoidance tool, methods for assessing the value of options in purchasing capital equipment, and the parameters of an effective asset-management program in which needless purchases and costs are avoided.

MINIMIZING THE IMPACT OF PAST AND FUTURE MISTAKES

The health care industry uses an extensive variety of costly capital equipment to treat disease and improve patient care. Not many would argue with the importance of most of this equipment, as millions of lives have been improved through using treatment technology enabled by current and historical capital-equipment purchases. Nonetheless, not all such purchases are of equal value. The truth is that health care organizations waste millions of dollars annually on equipment that is not needed, poorly used, or clinically unacceptable. These unwarranted purchases frequently fuel financial problems for an organization and can cause overall quality to spiral downward as it curtails future purchase of justifiable equipment.

Health care organizations waste millions of dollars annually on equipment that is not needed, poorly used, or clinically unacceptable.

Effective utilization research and management is the key in preventing these costly mistakes. The primary concept of utilization research is to quantify current and future use of equipment so that its value over time is maximized. Utilization may vary greatly from one piece of equipment to another but still be effective if the variables in usage are favorable to the health care organization. For instance, some equipment may be extremely profitable for an institution even though the actual day-to-day utilization of the equipment is quite low. On the other hand, equipment may lose money even when in constant use.

Utilization demographics can also change significantly over time. This is especially true in today's volatile marketplace, where reimbursement issues continue to be redefined year by year. In many cases, equipment is purchased to maximize revenues, which may nevertheless have changed significantly since the initial installation. Likewise, emerging technologies and treatment protocols often affect the use of equipment, making a replacement decision difficult to quantify. The health care organization

The primary concept of utilization research is to quantify current and future use of equipment so that its value over time is maximized.

should be extremely careful in approving replacement equipment because historical need may not be representative of best-practice treatment standards for the future. Reimbursement changes may likewise erode the rationale for continuing to treat patients using existing technology.

To understand these differences, it is critical that the health care organization spend the time adequately quantifying the utilization variables and also research the utilization effectiveness of existing equipment, as this list suggests:

Common Equipment Utilization Variables

Percentage of daily use	Repair history and up time	Age and remaining life cycle
Alternative treatment paths	Patient satisfaction	Shared usage
Upgrade path	Provider preference	Regulatory compliance
Condition of equipment	Operating hours and shifts	Strategic fit
Peak season and use variables	Location and ease of use	Essentiality
Demand forecasts	Clinical acceptance	Environmental issues
Reimbursement chain	Average patient wait time	Supply cost and availability
Number of like pieces of equipment	Future trends and changes	Training component
Functional value and options		Facility conditions
		Utilities

As the list demonstrates, there are many variables affecting utilization research. It is quite easy for an organization to make a mistake in purchasing equipment if the purchasing staff does not correctly address these issues. Utilization research also affects the long-term life-cycle cost of equipment. For instance, many organizations purchase copy machines based on crude estimates of the number of copies needed per month in a department or office. Unfortunately, a missized copy machine can be an expensive purchase mistake. A machine that is too small tends to need repairs frequently and significantly raise cost per copy. A machine that is too big and is underused represents overpurchase and a waste of capital-acquisition dollars. The same holds true for fax machines, computers, medical equipment, and similar capital-equipment purchases.

Many of the factors affecting equipment utilization are constantly changing. A common factor in increasing or decreasing use is adding new services to an area. This is of great importance because sometimes these changes represent strategic or competitive differences in the marketplace. Utilization forecasting is a difficult science that is made more complicated by biased opinions in the health care industry. For instance, a medical equipment vendor may push an organization to purchase equipment based on inflated estimates of projected utilization. The projection often comes in the form of census information depicting "need demographics" that may or may not match the patient demographics of the health care organization.

Utilization forecasting is a difficult science that is made more complicated by biased opinions in the health care industry.

Unfortunately, perceived need does not always translate into additional business, because there are many additional factors in whether offered services are used besides the presence of available equipment and treatment.

Census information may be correct in identifying need but incorrect in assuming that those patients are able and willing to receive the care when a health care provider offers it. Other health care providers may decide to get into the business as well, which lowers the overall utilization rate for everyone. Organizations should always be on the lookout for the opportunity to improve utilization whenever other providers decide to discontinue a treatment plan or service.

One of the best methods for dealing with these optimistic forecast variables is to assign a discount percentage rate that closely aligns the probability of patient and provider usage with historical usage rates achieved in similar projects. For example, history may show that these variables are skewed by 50 percent less utilization than what is normally projected by the vendor community. In this case, a pro forma would be constructed using half the vendor projections to estimate the profitability and viability of the new service or equipment purchase being considered.

Utilization is also greatly affected by the quality of the education and marketing process that promotes both new and existing treatment services. Referral paths among physicians and other providers often hinge on the level of active education that is given to these critical partners. This dynamic is true for internal providers as well. Changes in treatment method or choice should be communicated effectively to maximize the utilization of capital equipment. This list shows census-type issues that affect utilization within the health care community:

Census Dynamics Affecting Utilization

Population change	Marketing efforts	Competition
Treatment protocols	Community relations	climate
Facility openings and closings	Education programs	
Provider growth rate	Reimbursement changes	

PROCESS REENGINEERING
AS A PURCHASE-AVOIDANCE TOOL

Capital equipment is sometimes purchased to solve patient-care issues that are brought on by inefficient processes and poor management techniques. High or low equipment utilization is not always reflective of the real demand for its use. Sometimes demand forecasts can be skewed significantly if workflow issues or similar design variables are not addressed from a wide enough perspective. For instance, patient and physician scheduling models can greatly influence the efficiency of equipment utilization. Many health care organizations can significantly improve their financial performance by changing the dynamics of the work process itself, thereby eliminating bottlenecks, improving utilization standards, and lessening the need to purchase additional capital equipment.

Demand forecasts can be skewed significantly if workflow issues or similar design variables are not addressed from a wide enough perspective.

Process reengineering is an excellent purchase-avoidance tool. The concept has been successfully used by many industries to improve operations and reduce inefficiency and cost in every arena. Reengineering begins with thorough analysis of all the activities of a department or function, including the conceptual realities of what, why, and how the process is carried out to meet the demands of the customer groups. Once these dynamics are understood, then it is possible to move into a quantification phase, where outcomes are identified, measured, and reviewed to create a model of the actual events that characterize each subprocess element. These events can then be used as variables to be modified, eliminated, or changed to better improve the overall performance of the organization.

Event variables can be further defined and improved by understanding the limits of variation. Oftentimes employees can use a control chart to track variation in outcome and then use the measured quantities to help discover an underlying root cause or problem affecting maximum performance. For example, variations in the characteristics of the time frame for patient care delivery may be indicative of poor training, inadequate staff, low-quality supplies, functional obsolescence in facility design, and the like. Each variable can be quantified and studied through this statistically based process.

Process reengineering methodology also relies heavily on statistical analysis of time-related information variables. Time-related events are statistically mature and often afford a stable reference point for interpreting such data streams as patient turnover rate, drug or supply cost usage differences, and other economic data related to business and operational issues. Time events are usually expressed in terms of minutes, hours, days, years, and so on. These variables are also prone to be seasonal or cyclical in nature and usually contain many erratic components that must be tested, verified, and quantified to help accurately predict future outcomes.

Most of these variables can be expressed in terms of mathematical models or charted using common quantitative management tools. Once measured and quantified, the variables can be understood and stated as problems readily solved by health care professionals. Table 9.1 gives some common time-series components used in the statistical evaluation portion of process reengineering.

The dynamics of patient care are no less quantifiable than in any other industry. Some health care organizations mistakenly believe that physician care and similar provider services cannot be quantified as equipment issues can be. This is not so. In actuality, even differences among providers can be measured adequately if the parameters are defined well in the project study.

Although most of what occurs in a health care setting can be quantified and measured objectively, there are elements of any organizational climate that cannot be readily accounted for by these objective processes. For instance, political protocols, administrative bias, relationship dynamics, physician preference, and other subjective variables can significantly affect the viability of a health care organization. These subjective variables must be accounted for as well and addressed as part of the solution for any process reengineering effort.

Table 9.1. Common Time-Series Components

Term	Definition
Seasonal	Periodic recurring
Growth trend	Long-term growth
Linear trend	No growth, or decline
Cyclical	Nonconstant varied cycle
Declining trend	Long-term decline
Erratic	Consisting of random variables

Process reengineering techniques can also be used to redesign not only the internal structure of a department or treatment area but also the external flow of patients through the entire health care treatment network. These changes generally are cost-effective and streamlined; thus they tend to free up the primary providers and support staff to better serve the patient.

These analyses also support or invalidate the need for additional capital equipment or better technology. In many cases, an organization is indeed using an archaic practice that can be corrected most efficiently through automation or similar technology. Likewise, a practice that is inefficient may be tied to facility issues such as functional obsolescence, which is caused by adding services or tasks that were not designed into the original use or scope of the building.

HIDDEN CAPITAL-PURCHASE DOLLARS

Underused capital equipment often represents thousands of wasted resource dollars that can be put to much better use if the equipment is redeployed elsewhere or sold to generate additional revenue for the health care organization. A health care organization may allow capital equipment to go underused for years; it ends up wasting much of the useful life of the equipment in the process. This phenomenon is evident to some degree in most health care settings but is most evident in large institutions and especially common among organizations that have merged activities or been bought by another entity.

Merger and acquisition activities normally originate from a market-based financial analysis that demonstrates a positive correlation for growth and profitability by merging redundant practices and thereby eliminating waste and inefficiency in the market. The problem is that many of these ideals are better orchestrated in theory than in practice. It is a difficult task to merge two or more organizational structures. The probability of low utilization of equipment goes up significantly with the level of complexity of the merger or acquisition. Even organizations that are growing without the aid of a merger or acquisition are prone to creating inequity in equipment utilization thanks to the changing demographics of patient-treatment services facilitated by normal business growth.

Health care organizations should capture the hidden value of underused capital equipment and make of it an additional resource avenue to purchase other required capital equipment. It is critical to assess these issues continuously because idle equipment loses value day by day. Underused capital equipment also represents holding costs, which erode the financial viability of the organization. Among the holding costs associated with capital equipment are the following

A health care organization may allow capital equipment to go underused for years; it ends up wasting much of the useful life of the equipment in the process.

It is a difficult task to merge two or more organizational structures.

- Repairs

- Preventive maintenance

- Training and education

- Utilities

- Housekeeping and cleaning

- Supplies

- Facility upgrade and upkeep

- Property and facility use

- Staff support

ASSESSING THE VALUE OF OPTIONS

An effective utilization management and research program must include a process for assessing the value of options when purchasing capital equipment. This is a critical step in capital acquisition because equipment configurations can vary greatly even in the same product line. These variations can significantly affect the return on investment realized and also the future utilization of the equipment. Options can be both beneficial and detrimental, depending on the ultimate use of the equipment in the health care setting.

This ultimate-use scenario is key to effective utilization research. For instance, a CT scanner purchased for a hospital trauma center is likely to be configured with many more option packages than a scanner ordered for an outpatient diagnostic center. The trouble is that the vendor might still try to sell the unnecessary features to the outpatient center, resulting in a loss through idle technology. Equally bad is the hospital's purchase of the scanner minus many of the features required by the radiology staff. This underpurchase of technology will probably limit the revenue stream and lead to future purchase of the options at a greater price.

This is a common scenario in many health care institutions. Unfortunately, option packages purchased after the initial period tend to be much

Streamlining Health Care Operations

more expensive to buy and retrofit. They are usually much less costly when purchased as part of the original equipment configuration because the features are added during assembly at the factory, not in expensive field installation. Additionally, most of the leverage for price concessions and other manufacturer-related discounts and incentives is achieved during the initial purchase period, when the health care organization's negotiating strength is at its peak.

Equipment features, functions, and options should be assessed for utilization issues using the same methods as any other potential purchase. Each option should be quantified in terms of its life-cycle costs, reimbursement impact, treatment pathways, and strategic fit within the organization. If done correctly, these decisions become objective economic decisions that contribute to the future viability of the health care organization. On the other hand, option purchases resulting from nonquantifiable decisions (such as vendor preference, ease of purchase, allowable budget, and similar decisions) usually result in wasted capital-acquisition dollars.

Each option should be quantified in terms of its life-cycle costs, reimbursement impact, treatment pathways, and strategic fit within the organization.

Medical equipment configuration variability is similar to that seen in buying a new car. Most manufacturers have an entire line of cars, to fit every possible budget. Further, within each model line, there are even more configuration ranges. One model may come with cloth seats or leather seats, single or dual air conditioning, six-cylinder or eight-cylinder engine, and so on. The truth is that most of these additional options and features do not get you down the road any better than the base model does. This is true for equipment related to health care as well. Manufacturers often build in options and features that do little more than impress the future purchaser. Leather seats are nice, but they may be a nonreimbursable luxury.

ASSET MANAGEMENT REDEFINED

The typical health care organization has an asset-management program that is primarily an information repository used to track the maintenance and repair activities associated with its support equipment. It may use these data-collection activities to meet JCAHO (Joint Commission on the Accreditation of Healthcare Organizations) audit trail requirements or to track depreciation schedules for the financial services department. Although each function is important, this level of asset management does not provide the degree of coverage needed to prevent costly capital-acquisition issues or help much to increase utilization of equipment.

An effective asset-management program should prevent needless purchase of capital equipment and greatly lessen the need to rent, lease, or borrow equipment during peak usage periods. Further, the program should be comprehensive enough to permit identifying every asset and allow intelligent tracking of all the information necessary to optimize decisions regarding any capital purchase, repair, or replacement. Here are some key components in a comprehensive asset-management program:

Key Components of an Asset-Management Program

Physical inventory	Performance evaluation	Bar code and tag information
Maintenance history		
Model and manufacturer profile	Safety issues	Depreciation schedule
	Acquisition data	
Tracking mechanism	Total on-hand quantity	Disposal trail
Facility and construction brief		Age, condition, value
	History of theft or unusual loss	Contact information
Rental history		
Equipment location status	Repair history	

Equipment utilization is severely affected by the dynamics of immediate availability. Users often feel that they need additional equipment because it is not readily available when needed. Unfortunately, poor tracking mechanisms or unreliable location surveys can cause nonavailability. This is especially true for portable units, certain types of minor medical equipment, and even some major movable-equipment items.

Poor tracking and inventory methods lead to false representation of equipment utilization, which in turn often leads to unnecessary equipment purchase. The costs can be significant in some health care organizations. For instance, an organization that is renting a lot of IV pumps may find that its actual utilization is 50 percent less than perceived because many of the pumps may be out of circulation and not available to the health care units needing them.

Many organizations are solving these equipment utilization issues through installing extensive equipment-tracking technology that helps nursing and biomedical staff locate equipment when needed. These can be good tools, but the cost of the program often outweighs the benefit received. Such a program should be cost-justified just like any other purchase to see if the outlay is recoverable from normal business operation. In these financial reviews, as in all pro forma–based purchases, soft dollars should be ignored. Vendors often inflate the value of tools by imputing a dollar value for the nursing and staff time needed to locate the equipment. Most organizations never realize any cost savings from dollar values such as these (that is, soft dollars).

SUMMARY

Quantifiable justification for current and future use of equipment is necessary when implementing a sound utilization management plan that maximizes equipment usage over time. Very rarely is this demonstrated in the health care world today. Biases and politics, as well as general lack of utilization knowledge, are the reason. The health care industry, with its expensive capital purchases, should embrace utilization management whenever possible. Although utilization forecasting can be a complicated subject, particularly with the various parameters available within the health care setting, ignoring the subject is simply too costly.

Other industries have demonstrated the need for process reengineering as a purchase-avoidance tool. Health care can likewise benefit from the results of information gathered through the process of analysis that this technique permits.

An organization trying to find additional resources should search out underused capital equipment. The equipment is often better used elsewhere within an organization or sold to generate revenue. Particularly in a larger institution or in an organization that has merged with another provider, wasted equipment dollars can frequently be found and redirected.

Utilization management should embrace evaluation of capital-equipment options purchases. Each option should be appraised as a separate purchase, as in the case of any capital-equipment purchase. Correctly done, options can be objectively evaluated for their cost-effectiveness and organizational need.

Effective asset management should include the ability to prevent costly capital acquisitions within an organization. Too often, the asset-management program stops short of this goal.

QUESTIONS TO PONDER

1. Is your organization conducting utilization research to determine the actual need for current and future capital equipment?

2. How well are utilization variables quantified in the process of reviewing capital-equipment purchases?

3. Are future trends and changes in market conditions and reimbursement paths factored into the utilization demographics? If not, what steps should be taken to remedy this?

4. Do employees understand the need for utilization studies? To what degree are physicians or other provider groups educated on this process?

5. What percentage of historical purchases were conducted using statistically supported evaluation methods? Did these include utilization management factors?

6. How well is your organization tracking census data? Does this include facility openings and closings, marketing efforts, and community relations data?

7. Are process reengineering techniques used to solve patient-care issues? Have they been successful? What can be done to make them better?

8. If used, how effective have process reengineering techniques been in helping your health care organization avoid capital-equipment purchases?

9. How effective is your organization's process for assessing the value of options when purchasing major capital equipment?

10. How much equipment is not used or rarely used? Could these items be sold to generate additional capital-acquisition dollars?

11. Does organizational staff understand the capital-equipment holding costs associated with keeping underused equipment?

12. Are growth trends and other common time-series component variables used as benchmarking statistics to capture objective criteria from the organization's normal operations?

13. How effective is your organization's asset-management program? Does it include most of the key components listed in the chapter? If not, why not?

14. To what extent does the organization rent equipment to keep up with high demand? Are all of these costs justified? Do some of them reflect poor equipment tracking procedures?

CHAPTER 10

Equipment Service
Balancing Quality and Control

Today's health care leaders have many options for taking care of organizationally owned equipment. The market has shifted significantly in recent years and is now saturated with repair and service businesses of every conceivable size and sophistication. Ten years ago, original equipment manufacturers (OEMs) dominated the marketplace. This is no longer true, as independent service organizations (ISOs) have multiplied at a phenomenal rate and now number in the thousands nationally. This change in the service industry has created a marketplace where health care leaders can effectively shop around for the best-priced quality service available. Although choices and provider options abound, the health care leader needs to understand the dynamics of this industry and how to effectively control the cost of equipment maintenance and repairs.

Several major elements affect cost within the service arena. Surprisingly few health care organizations manage this area effectively; the result is inefficiency, increased cost, unnecessary outsourcing, and insufficient training. Careful analysis of the equipment service area often reveals a service-as-needed mentality, as opposed to proactive service planning along with negotiating service arrangements during the purchasing process. This type of neglect creates a deluge of waste and unnecessary expenditures across an entire organization. This chapter reveals these areas of waste, suggests means for driving out cost, and gives examples of how seemingly minor ineffi-ciencies can affect an organization's bottom line.

CREATE A MACRO APPROACH

Expense related to equipment service represents a high-cost area for any health care organization. Vendor repairs, service training, replacement parts, and installation costs often far exceed the initial capital-acquisition cost of equipment. Therefore it is imperative to look comprehensively at how equipment is maintained so as to maximize investment over time. The equipment service arena is complicated, and there are countless ways in which costs can skyrocket out of control. Unnecessary costs stem from a variety of factors: neglect, inappropriate reliance on vendor and manufacturer support, overservicing and underservicing, noncompetitive and unnecessary parts replacement, and unfocused training.

The equipment service arena is complicated, and there are countless ways in which costs can skyrocket out of control.

For equipment service to be cost-effective, it must be handled by step-ping back from the details of the process. This means that everything must be looked at in the overall context of how each individual cost driver affects other operating and capital-acquisition costs. Responsible individ-uals must understand the factors that drive equipment service cost and cre-ate an atmosphere in which service issues are strategically aligned with the long-term goals of the organization. This approach makes it much easier to decide on economical replacement time frame, type and extent of mainte-nance coverage, negotiated length of warranty, the criticality of mainte-nance-related training, and so on. Here is a list of common mistakes related to equipment service, made all the time by health care organizations in maintaining equipment:

Points of Failure in the Equipment Service Strategy

- Equipment is purchased by price, without validating reliability.

- Annual service agreements are arbitrarily signed with the equipment manufacturer.

- No comparison is made of the cost of service to be carried out by the manufacturer, independent service providers, or in-house biomedical or similar support staff.

- In-house service personnel are not trained to the same standard as outside providers.

- Discount rates on repair parts are not negotiated during the acquisition process.

- The cost of repair parts is not compared to that in the industry, and no process is in place to evaluate price concessions offered by the manufacturer or vendor.

- Manufacturers are not accountable to a standard of excellence and not required to reimburse the organization for poor performance.

- Equipment with little or no utilization is carried under a service agreement or plan.

- Vendors are not accountable to the organization for service rendered on equipment when conducting repairs, preventive maintenance services, or related service events.

- Historical trend information is not captured or used to track critical patterns.

- Comparison of service events is internalized, with no tie-in to industry data.

- Proper tools are not available for in-house personnel to service equipment.

- Service manuals, schematics, and other reference materials are not obtained during initial purchase.

- No asset management process is in place to track equipment location, age, usage, history, cost, and related issues.

ELIMINATE LITTLE POCKETS OF GREAT LOSS

The entire health care arena comprises innumerable pockets of variable cost that are usually not linked to a single department or area. Rather, the costs tend to overlap and expand with the daily business operations of the organization. Many of these pockets of cost go unchecked for years and are rarely seen as a problem because most seem relatively minor. The truth is that these seemingly small individual costs can add up to hundreds of thousands of dollars in annual waste if not managed correctly. One common pocket of loss is that of equipment upkeep that has no basis in strategic planning.

Seemingly small individual costs can add up to hundreds of thousands of dollars in annual waste if not managed correctly.

Upkeep costs and equipment values are directly affected by such decision factors as the average replacement time frame. This affects cost in a number of ways because the replacement time frame triggers such things as maintenance decisions, resale value, a lease-or-buy scenario, and other critical implementation points. For instance, a decision to replace fleet vehicles at sixty thousand miles probably avoids most major repairs and many service events (for example, brake and tire replacements) and might warrant use of a vehicle leasing contract instead of purchasing.

On the other hand, a decision to keep vehicles until they reach the eighty-thousand-mile mark may necessitate at least one tire change, brake job, air conditioning service, and major engine tune-up per vehicle. But this decision could result in increased cost for major engine or transmission overhauls or repairs. Thus without analysis it is impossible to know which choice for a fleet replacement time frame is more appropriate. Each scenario has to be studied to determine its probable total life-cycle cost. Each choice must likewise fit the long-term strategic goals of the organization.

As stated earlier, upkeep issues also affect resale value. To further demonstrate this factor, consider how fleet resale value is affected by the number of miles driven and the age and condition of the vehicles at the time of disposal. These issues are reflected in the cleanliness of the vehicle, the quality of the service records, and the sales ability of the individuals involved. In many cases, health care organizations place no emphasis on this aspect of vehicle disposal even though the quality of the process directly contributes to the annual operating cost of the business. This process should be handled just as proficiently as any other operation to maximize the ROI of the vehicle fleet.

An example of a proactive approach to vehicle service is a requirement to have a detailing vendor clean the carpets and upholstery, steam clean the engine, and wash and wax the vehicles to maximize their value before final resale. This approach alone can frequently augment disposal value by 10–15 percent. Additionally, stringent standards for vehicle upkeep and use often prevent unnecessary wear and tear if employees understand that auditing procedures are in place to fix responsibility for negligent vehicle care. These benefits can be maximized even further by outsourcing resale responsibility to a local used car dealership equipped with sales staff that can spend the time to gain the best sale price possible.

DRIVE OUT COST WITH PROJECT TEAMS

The fleet example demonstrates a common opportunity to find and control cost in every facet of operation. Many of these cost-avoidance opportunities can be found and corrected by a temporary project team given the authority to research waste and correct problems of this nature for the corporation. This can be an effective approach because teams can be assembled from subject matter experts in several cross-functional areas. Examples abound of team-focused cost-reduction projects:

Potential Team-Focused Maintenance and Cost-Reduction Projects

- Reproduction costs, copier maintenance, and related service

- Food service maintenance and repair

- Sharpening services for surgical tools and maintenance-related items

- Lawn service, grounds maintenance, and related upkeep

- Furniture repair, replacement, and maintenance cost
- Information equipment repair and service
- Phone replacement, installation, and maintenance-related cost
- Plumbing and fixture repair
- Heating and air conditioning service
- Fleet maintenance costs
- Review of cost of paper products (to include cups, plates, and bathroom products)
- Vending services
- Linen delivery service
- Small-package carrier costs (United Parcel Service, Airborne Express, Federal Express)
- Office supply costs
- Inventory control and holding costs
- Housekeeping services
- Transportation-related costs such as courier service
- Cost-effective methods for reducing property and equipment loss
- Projects aimed at lowering incidence of patient and provider injuries and claims

Additionally, local vendors, suppliers, and business partners can be relied upon to assist in this process. For example, an organization wishing to investigate the replacement process for fleet tires may not have someone on staff who understands the tire business well enough to effectively implement a sound policy for lowering annual cost. There are likely many issues involved in a cost-effective tire replacement policy that would be overlooked by the staff if not properly advised by someone with knowledge of that industry. A local expert may recommend a line of tires that is slightly more expensive initially, yet change the tread-wear guarantee from thirty thousand miles to sixty thousand miles, thus giving the organization twice the normal tire service life. Further, the expert might recommend that valve stems not be changed during the process, thus saving the organization an additional twenty dollars per incident. This type of assistance can be gained at no additional cost and ends up benefiting both organizations.

OUTSOURCING VERSUS INSOURCING

The decision to use in-house staff rather than external partners to maintain equipment should be based primarily on the strategic objectives of the organization and how service and maintenance issues affect the viability of patient care. When this approach is taken, the how-to of equipment maintenance becomes another business-related decision process that is executed in the most cost-effective and quality-conscious manner. This concept is important because critical maintenance-related decision paths can become buried under headings such as training, personnel and supply costs, or become easily postponed events that end up causing the organization to waste significant dollars annually.

Effective comparison between outsourcing and insourcing must begin with clear understanding of the total cost of equipment upkeep. Organizations often get into trouble with these issues because they have not correctly identified all of the total costs and therefore frequently underestimate both the cost and the value of well-maintained equipment. For instance, equipment that is marginally maintained has a higher total life-cycle cost than similar equipment that has been well maintained. On the other hand, some organizations have gone to the opposite extreme and overmaintained equipment to the point that service-related costs actually add unnecessary life-cycle cost. Neither scenario is cost-effective for a health care organization.

Outsource vendors often bid against in-house personnel and are able to show significant annual savings because they either intend to eliminate the unnecessary cost or plan to undermaintain the equipment, knowing that the actual costs of maintenance are camouflaged by seemingly unrelated purchase events. Equipment care and upkeep directly affect several arenas of cost that are usually not immediately visible to the organization:

user or provider dissatisfaction with equipment, reduced overall total useful life, high utility cost, frequent major parts replacement, high installation or deinstallation cost, and low disposal or resale value. Most costs of this type are never evaluated when making a decision on selecting outsource versus insource service.

These costs manifest themselves in a number of ways. For example, user or provider dissatisfaction with equipment caused by poor service leads to requested replacement of equipment sooner than necessary. This factor alone can contribute to hundreds of thousands of wasted purchase dollars annually. An organization can usually look back into annual purchase decisions to compile a history of replacement life cycles and compare them against those of similar users to see if purchasing inconsistencies exist. Likewise, replacements can trigger other cost events such as room upgrades and related installation costs. Each critical contributing factor must be analyzed to determine the total cost of maintaining equipment. Here is a list of issues to be considered when evaluating equipment upkeep costs:

Critical Variables Affecting Cost of Equipment Upkeep

Service interval	User satisfaction	Quality of upkeep
Experience of repairers	Training level of staff	Expected life cycle
Upgrade paths	Equipment reliability	Replacement parts
Trade-in, disposal value	Installation and deinstallation costs	Utility cost

Medical equipment repairs within our industry often end up being completed by service personnel from the manufacturing community, regardless of whether the health care organization has in-house repair staff or not. This is especially true for complicated repairs, and sometimes even for routine preventive maintenance, because the OEM frequently has more experience and greater depth of resources than in-house personnel. Unfortunately, these repairs can be costly—often unnecessarily so.

In a brief prepared for the author, Donald P. Koenig, the senior vice president of sales and marketing for Neodyme Technologies, a national service-maintenance review and management firm, offered an industry perspective* from his organization's experience with helping health care providers control and lower service-related costs.

Industry Perspective

Historically, the maintenance of capital equipment in hospitals has been paid through service contracts with OEMs. It was common knowledge that the price of the equipment was always negotiable but the service contracts were at a fixed price that increased every year. This began changing in the early 1980s as the Prospective Payment System and DRGs [diagnosis-related groups] were introduced, causing hospital management to look much closer at all expenses including maintenance.

In this same time period, the variety of service options for healthcare was proliferating. The most significant change was the increase in the number of ISOs for patient care equipment, which grew from a few hundred companies in 1980 to more than twenty thousand by 1995. This ISO growth introduced the first significant competition for the service dollar. Other service options used by hospitals include in-house biomedical/clinical engineering departments, maintenance insurance policies, and asset management programs.

These changes have placed market pressures on the service providers to provide better service at lower cost. Service providers are now also expected to provide detailed information for the hospital on the work they performed. The profit margins inherent to equipment service are substantial. Statistics have revealed that

---

* Excerpt from brief titled "Maintenance and Repair Expenses in the Healthcare Industry." Jan. 2000. Used with permission. Neodyme Technologies Corp., 903 Harvey Rd., College Station, TX 77840-3550.

repairs costing more than $2,000 are less than 3 percent of the total number of service events, yet they account for 38 percent of the total service cost.

One of the most critical areas requiring vigilance [is] the time and materials charges levied by service vendors. Potential discrepancies include duplicate invoices, hours worked, parts charges, missing credits, and overcharges. Several companies who market service contracts on their equipment have established pricing structures that appear to penalize customers for choosing to use service on a time-and-materials basis. These tactics are indicative of the complexity inherent to the service practices experienced by the healthcare industry. Fortunately, in today's environment, most hospitals have alternatives when it comes to choosing their service vendor, and the economic incentives are strongly encouraging them to do just that.

TRAIN FOR SAVINGS

Organizations frequently view in-house service-related training as added cost with little or no ROI. These training sessions are likely to be postponed or eliminated whenever budgets are tight. This response usually does not prevent the additional cost but rather moves it around, and in many cases increases it exponentially. Untrained or undertrained service personnel tend to spend more hours and more money fixing equipment than well-trained personnel do. These individuals are also far more likely to end up calling in an outside vendor to repair the equipment. Any of these events can add significant annual service-related cost. Training, too, affects the downtime of equipment and can cause revenue loss to the health care organization that is impossible to recover.

> *Untrained or undertrained service personnel tend to spend more hours and more money fixing equipment than well-trained personnel do.*

Training issues also affect judgment decisions in parts replacement, repair and replacement evaluation, and other issues affecting overall organizational cost. In some cases, repair personnel may guess at service-related issues and order replacement parts that do not fix the problem and are frequently unreturnable. This creates a costly trial-and-error approach to equipment repairs. These issues often go unresolved and unreported to upper management, thus creating a false or misleading repair cost history for the organization. Such issues can also contribute to provider or user dislike for a particular manufacturer's equipment that is unrelated to the actual quality of the product. Organizations that plan for and implement training find that these problems are lessened or eliminated.

PURCHASE REPAIR PARTS EFFECTIVELY

Organizations spend huge sums on repair parts every year, which are usually not accounted for as strictly as other purchases. This is often the case because parts purchases frequently occur in a period of duress or emergency. This is especially true for medical equipment that generates a lot of revenue or is critical for patient care. Usually these service events are loosely monitored and cost is secondary to expedient repair. Fortunately, these two issues do not have to be

Competition is the key that unlocks the door to reasonable parts prices.

mutually exclusive. A health care organization can have quick repairs done and obtain cost-effective parts replacement if the issues are preplanned and executed properly.

One of the first mistakes that an organization makes in dealing with repair parts is not always treating them as normal purchases. Repair parts are just as much a common commodity for sale in the marketplace as any other available product. Parts costs are extremely variable, and vendor pricing is directly proportional to the degree of competition and research afforded each transaction. The standard vendor answer is always the list price, unless some other factor forces them to concede a lower pricing structure or discount rate. Competition is the key that unlocks the door to reasonable parts prices. The vendor fully understands the purchaser's option of buying parts from other supply sources. Additionally, there are a variety of ways to increase competition even if the manufacturer or vendor appears to be the sole supplier of repair parts.

Discount rates on replacement parts should be negotiated when equipment is initially purchased so manufacturer offerings can be competitively leveraged against one another. For example, consider a health care organization replacing an angio suite with three vendors competing against each other for the final selection process. This is the perfect opportunity to ask vendors to extend a common discount rate for their parts. The discount rate can then be used to purchase all future repair parts from this vendor, and to establish a negotiating benchmark tool with other vendors.

Competition can also be introduced into this scenario by comparing each vendor's offerings to another independent supplier's discount rates. This method works even with separate part commodity groups because it demonstrates other industry pricing structures that are present in the marketplace. The health care organization should take full advantage of the leverage opportunity in any new equipment purchase arena. Even where this is not done during initial negotiations, it can still be successfully argued in the postpurchase period when the vendor or manufacturer is trying to make sure the sale has been handled satisfactorily. Some manufacturers may be willing to extend arbitrary discount rates to build strong partnership arrangements with the health care organization.

Component parts are often manufactured by other suppliers and may be available at lower cost from the original parts supplier or a third-party distributor. In many cases, the original major equipment supplier inflates individual parts costs from subcomponent suppliers to create a high-return revenue stream. Repairs are often the most profitable extension of their business. Introducing competition and price shopping for parts is an effective way to reduce the annual cost of repair parts.

Parts costs can also be reduced drastically through group purchase initiatives. Even regional partnership buying arrangements can greatly reduce the overall cost of repair parts if several health care organizations join forces to create a purchase volume that benefits everyone. This practice is common in other industries and can be created quickly by as few as two cost-conscious organizations. Additionally, comparison of historical price concessions on a regional or national basis often forces vendors to extend best pricing terms to everyone, even when negotiated separately. Open communications among health care organizations is cost-effective and beneficial for all.

Purchasing used parts from the secondary market can also significantly reduce the costs of repair parts. In many cases, entire systems can be purchased for less money than what the new parts cost. This can be especially cost-effective for repairs involving parts that are high-cost but generally trouble-free. Secondary-market used parts prices can also elicit competition and discount rates from sole-source vendors who might normally be unwilling to make price concessions. Fear of losing the sale to a used-market supplier often forces these suppliers to concede as well.

Some organizations may find that they have enough annual parts buying volume to justify hiring an extra person with the sole responsibility to research parts replacement costs and alternative repair or replacement options. This can be a cost-effective approach to fending off rising equipment repair costs. Such a person can be responsible for finding alternative sources of supply for each major piece of equipment in the health care organization to include secondary supply sources. A comprehensive database of alternative suppliers could then be relied upon for quick price comparison whenever emergency service events occur. The next list suggests how to deal with the cost-avoidance issues to be considered in setting up an effective initiative for purchasing repair parts:

> *Secondary-market used parts prices can also elicit competition and discount rates from sole-source vendors who might normally be unwilling to make price concessions.*

Repair Parts and Cost Avoidance

- Keep competition alive in purchase of repair parts by including secondary market participants, independent suppliers, third-party dealers, and manufacturers and vendors.

- Compare resale and disposal value to parts replacement value when replacing equipment that can be used to delay or prevent new parts purchases.

- Negotiate a discount rate for repair parts during the initial new equipment purchase.

- Get return parts guarantees in writing before purchasing from vendor.

- Don't automatically buy when faced with a repair decision, as vendors may be willing to repair at little or no cost if handled as part of a future purchase decision or if warranted by extenuating circumstances (such as unreliable equipment or repair parts).

- Find out if the manufacturer supplies a toll-free phone line or similar dial-up service function that can be accessed by in-house service personnel (often automatically discounted to the service vendor community).

- Call the manufacturer for repair advice before calling in a service representative.

- Request extended warranty on repair parts in case the issue resurfaces in the future (eliminate repetitive repairs from unreliable parts).

- Seek cooperative purchase arrangements with other health care providers in the area.

- Involve sales representatives in repairs (this may lead to additional discounts or free service).

- Have technical staff request work-around solutions to fix the problem.

- Consider adding staff to research parts replacement solutions.

PREVENT LOSING MONEY IN BACKUP SYSTEMS

Most health care leaders probably understand the need to eliminate service contracts for backup equipment that is not used regularly, but some may not realize the full extent of waste when other important cost factors are weighed in the analysis. Much medical equipment is kept in reserve as insurance against the possible breakdown of a primary piece of equipment. This extra insurance status may actually cost the health care organization much more than just the annual maintenance and upkeep normally claimed by the department or unit demanding a backup system.

One big hidden-cost area is the lost revenue from timely sale of used equipment. The resale market for used medical equipment is a highly volatile one, constantly changing and heavily affected by both the age and condition of equipment and the emergence of alternative replacements in the new and used markets. Even a year's difference in the age of the equipment can account for a large change in resale dollar value in the secondary market. Delays in selling used equipment can end up costing the health care organization thousands of dollars in lost revenues.

Delays in selling used equipment can end up costing the health care organization thousands of dollars in lost revenues.

Closely related to this problem is the lost potential of using the backup equipment to fulfill other health care provider needs. In many cases, medical equipment that becomes obsolete for one type of care may in fact be perfectly acceptable for other treatment applications that require less-sophisticated technology. What frequently happens in a health care organization is that backup systems remain virtually unused even when other areas of care may be lacking adequate equipment. Correcting this imbalance in equipment utilization by redistributing medical devices can help the organization avoid purchasing equipment unnecessarily. This tactic can create more long-term savings than are realizable by simply selling the used equipment. In other words, the cost-avoidance potential of using the equipment to stave off purchasing frequently outweighs the resale value of the equipment.

Backup systems may also account for unnecessary training sustainment cost, utility cost, and nonrecoverable repair parts replacement and inventory holding costs. These areas of cost can be quite substantial and are usually hidden under a budget umbrella, making them difficult to find and fix unless preventive measures are put in place to stop this organizational hemorrhage.

Arguments for keeping backup systems usually revolve around providers' and users' nonquantifiable concern for uninterrupted patient care. There is often a perceived need to ward off any potential threat to equipment availability regardless of the cost to the organization. This is not good business practice; backup equipment insurance should be assessed in the same manner as any other type of insurance, so that the organization pays only for the level of protection actually needed. Careful analysis of need may reveal several opportunities for lowering the risk of nonavailable equipment: temporary rental agreements, alternative delivery sites for patient care, extended treatment hours (perhaps to make better use of similar equipment), and so on.

> *Arguments for keeping backup systems usually revolve around providers' and users' nonquantifiable concern for uninterrupted patient care.*

Additionally, analyzing need often demonstrates that equipment downtime amounts to temporary provider discomfort rather than lost business. This is frequently the case when service providers are readily available and can respond to malfunctions within a reasonable time. Medical equipment failure, like other equipment maintenance problems, usually occurs in a predictable pattern that can be remedied rather quickly by a well-trained service repair staff. Therefore it is imperative that the health care organization (1) spend time adequately researching the real need of any backup system, (2) support only those backup systems that are clearly needed, and (3) eliminate the cost of supporting those that do not pass the quantifiable test. Here is a list of key elements to look for in validating the need for a backup system:

- Reliability of the primary unit

- Current and historical downtime

- Level and quality of service support

- Availability of repair parts

- Criticality of the equipment to the mission

- Alternative equipment resources

- Total cost to maintain a backup system

- Patient and provider rescheduling options

IMPLEMENT STRATEGIC AND PROCEDURAL CHANGES FOR COST AVOIDANCE

There are a number of ways in which an organization can significantly lower annual operating expenses by improving day-to-day procedures. Opportunities for cost avoidance through procedural change can be found everywhere within the health care community, including the equipment service area. It can be uncovered by analyzing the cause-and-effect issues surrounding equipment wear and tear and then linking these causes back to cost-effective preventive processes that limit the frequency and severity of future service-related events. Most repairs can be eliminated or significantly postponed by applying a few well-orchestrated preventive initiatives.

Most repairs can be eliminated or significantly postponed by applying a few well-orchestrated preventive initiatives.

As an example of this, consider the success that the UPS has experienced in extending the useful life of its delivery truck fleet. In many instances, UPS has been able to double the normal life span of individual trucks by instituting an aggressive preventive maintenance program that minimizes the probability of failure. Frequent oil changes, tire rotation, safety checks, diagnostic analysis, battery and charging system checks, and systematic monitoring of fluid levels and similar measures extend the life of this critical fleet of vehicles and significantly lowers the annual operating and replacement cost as well. The results did not happen by accident; rather, they reflect strategic application of an operating plan that exists to reduce long-term cost and improve the quality and reliability of package delivery service to the end customer.

This approach can work within the health care community as well. Unfortunately, most health care organizations treat service as a routine cost and do not apply any strategic objectives to this critical support area. Cause-and-effect issues are rarely quantified, studied, or prevented. Service bills are typically treated as routine and nonnegotiable facts of business that happen sporadically and must be dealt with case by case. This style of equipment service and maintenance tends to be the most costly and has considerable impact on the profitability of the health care institution. Many organizations claim to have premier service programs in place because they outsource the maintenance service and support functions to an outside service provider. In most cases, the external maintenance providers are no more strategically oriented than the health care provider and represent only adequate maintenance support, in contrast to the strategic maintenance support demonstrated in the UPS example.

> *Cause-and-effect issues are rarely quantified, studied, or prevented.*

Countless other procedural and strategic changes can be implemented to help health care organizations control service cost and increase equipment life span and resale value. The entire health care community can improve these factors by employing best-practice research methods to every facet of service and maintenance operations. The next list contains some additional areas of procedural change and strategic adjustment that should be considered when evaluating the strength of a service-related program.

- Wear-and-tear analysis. Are patient-treatment procedures conducted in a manner that maximizes efficient use of the equipment (cost, procedure appropriate for type, and long-term "highest and best use" of equipment, as we shall see in the next chapter)?

- Diagnostics. Are maintenance survey tools and procedures appropriate for the level of sophistication and frequency of repair (remote diagnostics capability, self-actuated tests using software, and so on)?

- Training. Is the level of training of everyone concerned consistent with cost-avoidance goals (technical user training, provider applications training, maintenance and service support training)?

- Supplies and repair parts. Does the quality of consumable supplies and repair parts support the organization's long-term goals for readiness and equipment life cycle?

- Calibration. Can calibration procedures be automated, self-actuated by the equipment, or completed through use of external calibrating devices?

- Manufacturer responsibility. Are issues handled adequately by the manufacturer, with concessions negotiated for disputable matters (such as loaner equipment or free repairs)?

MAINTAIN FLEETS APPROPRIATELY

Every aspect of health care operations affects the profitability and viability of the organization, including fleet maintenance management. Frequently fleet service, upkeep, and repair depend on the individual care that the unit manager or department offers for each vehicle. An absence of general oversight in this arena often leads to excessive cost to the organization. These additional costs stem from such issues as driver abuse, inappropriate care and maintenance, nonstrategic purchasing and resale, nonnegotiated service, haphazard fueling practices, and many similar problems.

For example, oil and tire changes and routine maintenance events can end up costing the organization thousands of dollars annually and are frequently not managed globally. Small decision points, such as the frequency of oil change, can create variable cost structures that nickel-and-dime a health care organization into financial ruin. As the saying goes, a small leak can sink a great ship; it can likewise sink an otherwise solid health care provider. (Exhibits 10.1 and 10.2 illustrate variables in decisions that might contribute to unnecessary annual cost).

Small decision points, such as the frequency of oil change, can create variable cost structures that nickel-and-dime a health care organization into financial ruin.

The oil change service problem probably represents even more cost than necessary, considering that many organizations do not prenegotiate any such maintenance costs with the service provider. The cost of the oil change may be twice what it would be if the total number of annual oil changes needed by the organization is negotiated up front, and with two common providers. Imagine the difference in negotiating oil changes with a local garage if, up front, the potential annual volume is identified as 150 instead of one or two.

SUMMARY

Equipment servicing is an area that receives little attention within most health care organizations, despite the hidden costs associated with mismanaging this area. Although great pains may be taken in the initial purchase of equipment, it is unfortunate that the future servicing of such equipment is often handled without regard to weighing insourcing versus outsourcing, analyzing the complete life cycle as it pertains to servicing, identifying the cost of replacement parts, and facing the necessity and advantages of training.

Exhibit 10.1. Sample Annual Variable Costs for Fleet Maintenance

Number of vehicles	30
Average annual miles each	15,000
Total average miles	450,000

Oil change every **3,000** miles = 150 oil changes annually
   (at $20 each = $3,000)

Oil change every **5,000** miles = 90 oil changes annually
   (at $20 each = $1,800)

Tires replaced at **30,000** miles = 15 tire changes annually
   (at $400 each = $6,000)

Tires replaced at **45,000** miles = 10 tire changes annually
   (at $400 each = $4,000)

Engine tune-up at **30,000** miles = 15 tune-ups annually
   (at $150 each = $2,250)

Engine tune-up at **45,000** miles = 10 tune-ups annually
   (at $150 each = $1,500)

Brake service at **45,000** miles = 10 brake services annually
   (at $150 each = $1,500)

Brake service at **60,000** miles = 7.5 brake services annually
   (at $150 each = $1,125)

Air conditioning service at **30,000** miles = 15 air conditioning services annually
   (at $200 each = $3,000)

Air conditioning service at **45,000** miles = 10 air conditioning services annually
   (at $200 each = $2,000)

(Total differential annual variable cost for these five basic services = $5,325)

Exhibit 10.2. Sample Annual Variable Costs for Fleet Fuel

Number of vehicles	30
Average annual miles each	15,000
Total average miles	450,000

Assuming 25,000 gallons of fuel used annually
(450,000 divided by average of 18 mpg)

Nonnegotiated prices	Negotiated prices
Regular unleaded $1.05 = $26,250	Regular unleaded $1.00 = $25,000
Midgrade unleaded $1.16 = $29,000	Midgrade unleaded $1.09 = $27,250
High-grade unleaded $1.24 = $31,000	High-grade unleaded $1.14 = $28,500

(Total differential annual variable cost for fuel = $6,000)

The health care organization must make equipment upkeep a strategically planned area. Arbitrary decisions are often made in regard to replacement and upkeep costs, and this translates into unaccountable losses. No doubt few executives realize that the costs associated with equipment servicing gradually compound, to adversely affect the efficiencies being created in other areas of the organization. Areas such as fleet management, timely resale of equipment to obtain best value, and comparative analysis are important if the organization is to remain viable.

Project teams, comprising in-house personnel, local vendors, and business partners, should be used to effectively drive out costs. Additionally, calling upon expert advice in maintaining equipment is highly effective and can reveal hidden areas of waste. Careful attention should also be given to whether equipment is maintained by the manufacturer or by trained in-house personnel. Training inefficiencies and how they affect the organization can be lessened through appropriate analysis of the benefits of spending training dollars.

Purchasing repair parts needs to be done in a way that precludes emergency part replacement—a commonplace inefficiency in many health care organizations. Such management obviously does not work in favor of best pricing, or even decent pricing. Rather, discount pricing should be negotiated as frequently as possible, and comparative manufacturer pricing should be weighed. By introducing competitive pricing, group purchase initiatives, selection of used equipment, and other innovative policies into the parts replacement process, a new degree of savings can be realized.

Inefficient use of older equipment should be analyzed as well. The viability of using such equipment as a type of insurance against main system failure should be reviewed in terms of necessity, the cost of not reselling the used equipment, and the potential for the used equipment to be used in another place within the organization.

QUESTIONS TO PONDER

1. Are service-related events strategically aligned with the long-term goals of your organization?

2. How involved are maintenance personnel in purchase and capital-acquisition decisions?

3. To what degree have vendor performance and equipment reliability standards been used to track critical ROI issues?

4. Have upkeep costs and equipment replacement time frames been closely monitored to reduce the risk of technological obsolescence?

5. Are multidisciplinary project teams used to drive out costs?

6. What decision process is used to determine the direction of maintenance service for the organization? Does this include review of outsourcing versus insourcing opportunities?

7. Are in-house maintenance and service personnel trained to the same standard of expertise as workers in the manufacturing community of service providers? If not, why not?

8. Is training viewed as a cost-driver or a cost-saver?

9. Have all cost variables in critical equipment upkeep been identified and fully minimized?

10. What process is in place to track effective purchase of replacement repair parts? Have historical purchases been validated to ensure cost-competitive resourcing?

11. How frequently are replacement parts purchased from secondary market providers?

12. Are all backup systems reviewed to ensure that minimum equipment utilization goals are met and that all hidden costs are correctly identified?

CHAPTER 11

Major Projects

Cost-Effective Expansion and Growth

ealth care organizations that are involved in expansion and growth through major projects invariably find that the end cost far exceeds the original budgetary analysis. Justification for going over budget has become commonplace, despite the current nationwide demand for more efficiency. Rather than accepting this reality as the status quo, project managers must understand the dynamics of realistic expectations and be able to keep projects on track.

This chapter describes commonsense ways to keep often-complicated projects within budgetary confines. It is not necessary to be an expert in construction to be an effective project manager, but it is important to understand the construction process. This includes familiarity with the bidding process and various regulatory specifications, and emphasizing saving money through appropriate technology assessment and implementation.

MANAGE THE SCOPE OF THE PROJECT

It is amazing how quickly project budgets can be exceeded if not managed comprehensively. The reason this often happens is that costs naturally expand as new ideas, personalities, methods, and energies are introduced into the project. The truth is that project construction and expansion costs are extremely variable, and any number of potential everyday decisions can wreak havoc on budget parameters. Opinions and input from interested parties can vary greatly, and this variance in the appropriate direction or selection alternatives can spell a large change in the actual scope and cost of a potential project. Therefore, the organization must understand this dynamic and plan appropriately to prevent escalating project costs.

The health care organization must exercise due caution and restraint in attempting to expand or grow business in today's highly volatile marketplace. Good revenue-enhancing ventures adhering to initial projected cost sometimes become poor-performing ventures as the scope of the original project is abandoned or exceeded. It is critical to assess the potential variability of a project from both profit variable-cost perspectives. Financial pro formas should be completed that show the break-even cost points and the high and low performance return points determined by the specified needs of the venture under consideration. These financial benchmarks then become the anchors for the project that help to keep ideas, suggestions, and changes in line with the original scope agreed on by the leaders and support staff.

If handled correctly, changes and recommendations from project partners can actually decrease overall costs, thus making the project more profitable than first imagined. Valuable input from others can improve the overall quality of the project as well. This is especially true if the suggestions and recommendations are made early in the project planning process. Budgets are often exceeded because unforeseen "essentials" have not been planned for appropriately; once the budget is set, these unforeseen issues either become budget breakers—or quality breakers—as other important aspects of the project sometimes have to be downsized or eliminated to make room for necessary changes. Again, each of these decisions become project scope changes that may reflect poorly on the overall revenue enhancement goals of the health care organization.

Although some changes are unavoidable, most can be prevented with proper planning and control. The best way to prevent changes from being costly is to make all of them on paper before the project begins and then lock in the design so that none of the participants can make arbitrary changes without approval from the entire team. This prevents many of the

Streamlining Health Care Operations

moment-by-moment, emotionally driven changes that often creep into a project unnoticed by participants. Project members are predictably surprised to find that costs have exceeded budgetary amounts because many of the seemingly small changes end up costing more than anticipated.

As an example of this in practice, imagine the difference in project cost if someone suggests a seemingly simple change to the size or design of a door. During the initial planning session, it might involve only a small erasure and update to the preliminary drawing or architectural design. Changes at this stage probably have little effect on the overall budget planning process.

If the change is made just prior to installation, then the cost includes additional charges from both the door supplier and the contractor. In this case, the supplier probably charges extra for restocking the door, plus adding the difference in price for the new door. Additionally, the contractor or subcontractor is likely to charge a higher rate to install the new door because the cost is calculated as a separate project, as opposed to work done as part of the original bid for the scope of work already agreed upon. Although not ideal, these changes are often manageable, especially if they rarely occur or involve simple changes.

The best way to prevent changes from being costly is to make all of them on paper before the project begins and then lock in the design so that none of the participants can make arbitrary changes without approval from the entire team.

Now consider the case of a change made after installation. The cost of replacing the door is exponentially greater than the original installation. If the original door has already been installed, then it probably cannot be returned to the supplier. If the new door is of a different size, then the framing and construction already completed have to be removed and redone to accommodate the new change. In this instance, the actual price difference of changing one door can easily end up adding several thousand dollars to the cost of the project. Unfortunately, expansion projects often involve hundreds of seemingly small changes that waste millions in financial resources every year.

As each example demonstrates, it is much more cost-effective to make changes early in a project. If changes are warranted, it is best to make the decisions during the planning or design phase so that they are captured on paper and in drawings. Generally speaking, the earlier the change is decided, the less the cost to the overall project. Changes made early rarely affect the viability of other portions of the project, thus allowing quality to remain high while satisfying the expansion objectives of the health care organization.

USE BUDGET CONTROL MECHANISMS

Project budgets should always be tied to the scope of the project. Although this statement may seem trite to some, health care organizations frequently allow project budgets to continue to expand as interested parties demand additional equipment, square footage changes, better material, and other similar concessions to satisfy goals that may be contrary to the original intent specified in the project scope. Budget control mechanisms help to alleviate these problems and guide project leaders in staying within the dollar limits established during the initial financial analysis and review.

Project budgets should always be tied to the scope of the project.

Budget control tools include detailed cost estimates and cost estimate summaries for each major portion of the project. Estimates should include

- Construction costs
- Supply and equipment costs
- Contractor and subcontractor labor costs
- Architecture design and planning costs

- Permitting and regulatory compliance costs

- Environmental compliance costs

- Legal fees

- Insurance coverage

- Furniture and interior design costs

- Landscaping or grounds costs

- Project consulting costs

- Any other potential fees or services that directly or indirectly affect the total cost of the project

Budget control mechanisms should also include project completion schedules, detailed descriptions of materials, building checklists, a master plan that outlines the preapproved scope of the project, and an aggressive plan for reducing project costs throughout the execution of the expansion or growth project. Detailed budget control tools such as these significantly reduce the variability of project costs and hold everyone accountable for staying within the budget parameters needed to meet the financial goals of the health care organization.

Contractors and subcontractors do not always concern themselves with the best supply prices because they intend to pass the costs onto the customer.

Project leaders should be aggressive in saving project dollars. There are a variety of ways that budgets can be controlled to maximize savings and positively affect the overall quality of the project. Material and equipment pricing, for instance, can vary extremely even among identical items. Contractors and subcontractors do not always concern themselves with the best supply prices because they intend to pass the costs onto the customer.

Project leaders should also watch contractors and suppliers to make sure they do not substitute lower-quality material for higher-quality.

In many cases, it is better for the health care organization to provide the supplies and equipment or else work closely with the contractor to ensure a competitive environment is maintained so that the contractor does not get lazy in estimating costs and controlling expenses. Project leaders should also watch contractors and suppliers to make sure they do not substitute lower-quality material for higher-quality. This is especially possible with air conditioning units and other critical large components, where the total cost of the mistake may not surface until later, with higher utility bills or more expensive service and maintenance costs. There are several elements in an effective control process:

Budget Control Tools and Processes

Project outline and scope	Statistical bidding-process	Committee accountability
Building checklist	Repair history audits	Time and event schedules
Energy use audits	Predesign and design phases	Landscaping plan
Expert advisory council	Furniture checklists	
Equipment checklists	Cost estimate checklist	
Cost estimate summary	Purchasing agent	

Budgets can also be exceeded rather easily if the original scope of work is not correctly aligned with the regulatory requirements of the construction industry. Health care organizations often receive contractor bids for expansion projects that have not been tested against all of the requirements imposed by regulatory bodies, permitting entities, inspection authorities, and other interested parties. Overlooking them may have quite an impact on the total cost of construction. The bidding contractor may know that the plans do not meet the guidelines but bid anyway.

Unfortunately, some contractors practice this type of bidding procedure because they can improve their profit margins with add-on requirements. For example, assume a project plan was approved and bid upon without having been signed off by the local fire safety commission. Later, the fire marshal may require any number of additional require-

Health care organizations often receive contractor bids for expansion projects that have not been tested against all of the requirements imposed by regulatory bodies, permitting entities, inspection authorities, and other interested parties.

ments that must be met to obtain a certificate of occupancy for the building. Additional fire safety add-ons might include upgraded sprinkler systems, electronic fire alarm systems, mechanical roof and smoke vents, and additional exit doors. Changes such as these can add hundreds of thousands of dollars to an expansion project. It is important for the health care organization's project leaders to be cognizant of local regulatory requirements and to closely monitor all bids for compliance. The components of an effective bid process include

- Competitive environment
- Clear specifications
- Regulatory input
- Multiple participants
- Prequalified bidders

- Minimum-and-maximum variables
- Defined responsibilities
- Written expectations
- Quality assurance review

INDEX COSTS TO OTHER INDUSTRIES

The health care industry has many unique building requirements and regulatory guidelines that significantly affect the cost per square foot of construction and expansion projects. Nevertheless, much of what is done in the health care arena is no more complicated or costly than any other building or construction project. Unfortunately, for some aspects of health care the high cost per square foot of construction often shows up in the areas of construction that should not be reflective of the higher cost ratios. For instance, a health care organization may have spent $135 per square foot to construct a surgical suite and agree to a $75 cost per square foot to build a physician office building. On the surface, this reduction in price seems reasonable, until one compares the cost of the physician office building space with other office-related construction. If the going rate of construction for general office use is $40 per square foot, then the $75 price is excessive and unwarranted.

Unfortunately, for some aspects of health care the high cost per square foot of construction often shows up in the areas of construction that should not be reflective of the higher cost ratios.

This practice is actually quite common in the health care industry. Health care organizations often rely on builders who construct only medical-related projects. They often hire more expensive labor pools and maintain special staff to support the design and build of complicated medical buildings. Unfortunately, the higher paid staff and specialty firms are often the same ones that show up to build the lesser projects as well. The health care organization frequently pays a premium price for construction that is no better than what can be obtained through a standard construction company at a much lower price.

Likewise, material costs and supplies are often billed at higher rates. For this reason, a health care organization should make it common practice to test these costs against other industries to validate the price and quality received. The next list outlines some of the common construction areas that should be indexed against other industries to validate cost appropriately:

A health care organization should make it common practice to test these costs against other industries to validate the price and quality received.

Common Areas of Construction-Cost Variance Among Industries

Architecture design	Insulation	Flooring and tile
Masonry	Framing	Heating and air conditioning
Landscaping	Concrete	ditioning
Excavation	Roofing	Drywall and
Trim and finish work	Equipment	sheetrock
Signage	Consulting	Environmental work
Engineering	Phone systems	Interior design
Information systems	Electrical	Contracting and
Plumbing	Cabinetry	service

CONSIDER "HIGHEST AND BEST" USE

Health care organizations often waste valuable real estate by putting low-volume or low-revenue return services into high-cost construction areas. This practice in turn leads to unnecessary additional construction fees in high-cost areas to accommodate emerging medical services. For instance, a hospital may be housing rehab services in an area that can be used for out-patient surgeries. This could be a very expensive trade of real estate because the rehab services may easily go into a building or area that does not cost much to build or remodel. Likewise, the surgical area is a costly construction project because it requires medical gases, special monitoring, higher grade electrical apparatus, better ventilation systems, and similar high-cost items.

Sometimes the highest and best use of a space cannot be realized until staging operations are put in place to correct other historical mistakes or practices in usage.

In the health care industry, some services are constantly being eliminated while others are growing, creating inequity in the organization's use of real estate. This is especially true for older health care systems and medical centers that have a long history of continuous service in the industry. The next list outlines usage aspects that must be considered when realigning health care services with an organization's real estate.

Highest and Best Use Planning Considerations

- Revenue-generation value of the space
- Efficient use of space and work areas
- Patient-use considerations
- Construction retrofit costs
- Existing construction, utility, infrastructure
- Correlation and use of accessory equipment
- Mechanical and electrical requirements
- Cost of domino effect (changing use)

Sometimes the highest and best use of a space cannot be realized until staging operations are put in place to correct other historical mistakes or practices in usage. These corrections often involve placing some services in a temporary facility or condition until all of the infrastructure issues can be resolved. These temporary conditions (the domino effect mentioned in the preceding list) can be costly as well and should be analyzed carefully to make sure that the losses do not outweigh the gains. Obviously, consideration must also be given to the comfort, convenience, and care of the patient populace served by the current and future space.

ALLOW FOR GROWTH: DON'T BUILD FOR GROWTH

Expansion projects frequently center on future goals and objectives of the health care organization in reaching an emerging patient group that is expected because of census changes in the region or other demographic aspects (aging populace, growth rate in number of reported cancers, or similar evidence). The problem with expansion projects of this type is that predictions of growth may not materialize quickly enough to support the cost of construction, utilities, and infrastructure upkeep once the project is completed. For this reason, it is essential that the health care organization carefully construct any expansion project so that the growth goals can be met without sacrificing the short-term financial health of the institution.

This objective is best achieved by constructing what is clearly supportable from today's financials while simultaneously putting into place the infrastructure to support a quick and complete build-out as needed. For instance, a new expansion project might be drawn up as needed for the future but then built in phases corresponding to the growth patterns needed to meet patient care needs. Some aspects of the expansion project may involve putting in the plumbing, electrical, and support functions necessary to sustain future development, without actually completing the finished portion. Additionally, it may make sense to build a virtual shell for future space without committing to equipment installation, plumbing fixtures, or expensive flooring or finish. Or space can be created as oversized utility closets, lounges, and other inexpensive real estate earmarked for change into space for additional equipment or procedure use in the future.

COMPARE OFF-SITE AND ON-SITE COST

A number of variables affect the cost of expansion in medical facility construction. One of the biggest factors affecting construction cost is the regulatory add-on requirements facing many hospitals and health care organizations: architectural design reviews, minimum construction specifications, engineering studies, environmental impact studies, and patient bed or procedure licensing regulations. Oftentimes these additional costs are primarily factors affecting the cost of expansion projects linked to the hospital facility. Sometimes the critical factor is whether the construction is deemed inpatient or outpatient service and where the services will be located (that is, attached to the hospital or completely separate).

In many instances, the cost of constructing a needed facility can be significantly lowered if it is built separately from the main edifice. Reimbursements received are sometimes also strictly linked to the placement of the facility. These variables strongly suggest that the financial viability of a project could be threatened by placing it within the health care facility rather than locating it in an off-site location. Pro formas should always be prepared to demonstrate this relationship between the cost of construction needed to place services internally against the cost to place the same services off site. Additionally, planning initiatives should also focus on combining construction objectives with outreach or projection goals as well. For instance, locating the new facility within the confines of the area with the highest projected patient demographic growth may be better from both financial-performance and patient-access perspectives.

EXAMPLES OF CONSTRUCTION COST VARIABLES

Commercial real estate professionals know that the best way to ensure a profitable enterprise is to build only what is needed to sell to others in the marketplace. The degree of quality and features built into a project must be reflective of the prevailing market conditions. The extra cost of beautiful features—such as marble floors and fancy trim, lighting, and fixtures—often cannot be recovered from buyers and ends up costing builders and investors lost profit. Accordingly, the health care organization needs to be careful not to build an expansion project that exceeds the level of reimbursement or revenue flow that is required to sustain it in the future. Much of what is built in the United States today suffers from too many extras in building expense, construction costs, and unnecessary equipment purchases.

The extra cost of beautiful features— such as marble floors and fancy trim, lighting, and fixtures— often cannot be recovered from buyers and ends up costing builders and investors lost profit.

Construction cost variables are infinite and foreseeable. Realistically speaking, practically every aspect of a construction project contains variables of cost. Carpets can range from $1.99 to $35 a square yard (or more). The truth is, every cost is variable— including the seemingly solid costs of concrete, mortar, lumber, and sheetrock. For every figure paid, there are countless examples of others that could have been paid for essentially the same product. Even the time of year can greatly affect construction prices. Slow building periods normally entail lower labor and supply costs, while the busy season typically causes prices to skyrocket. With every business, supply and demand affects the total cost of construction for everyone.

For this reason, it is critical that the health care organization clearly define the pro forma objectives for the finished project and put processes in place that tie daily construction and purchase decisions to the overall goals of the organization. This way, decisions affecting cost and quality can be solved within the right framework of profit accountability. Competition may dictate that some luxury features are necessary and prudent in order to meet the overall objectives of the project. However, it is always possible to add a few special touches to a construction project without breaking the bank in doing so. A careful selection-and-control process allows decision makers to add what is necessary without sacrificing the profit potential of the expansion project. Here is a lengthy sampling of supply variables affecting construction costs:

Common Variables in Cost of Construction Supplies

Carpet (foam padding, glue)

Use of color coordination

Roofing (type, style, color)

Amount and type of landfill

Wallpaper (style and width)

Tile (type, color, texture)

Trim (plastic, wood, metal)

Cabinetry (standard or built-in)

Fixtures (standard or custom)

Drywall (length, texture)

Windows (style, insulation)

Lighting (style, use, power)

Insulation (r-factor, sound)

Waterproofing (climate, use)

Paint (color, life, type)

Plumbing (copper, PVC)

Heating, ventilation, and air conditioning (life, power, use)

Grading, hours of operation

Doors (style, width, locks)

Concrete blocks (size, shape)

Pest control (type, extent

Landscaping (type, style)

Flooring (wood, tile, vinyl, linoleum)

Concrete (thickness, type)

Stairs (standard or custom)

Framing (wood or metal)

Borders (style, width, color)

Footings (depth, type, form)

Appliances (type, style, use)

Gutters (metal, plastic, use)

Note that factors such as "use of color coordination" affect cost because they influence other selection decisions.

The list gives a picture of the infinite choices available in making construction decisions. Within each of these common examples and the many others not listed, it should be readily apparent that control is needed at every stage of the construction project. As an example of this, consider the cost difference that window selection has on a construction project. Windows come in every imaginable shape, size, and configuration. They also determine the future utility cost of a facility. Air conditioning and heating requirements can be greatly affected by the insulation value of windows. A double- or triple-insulated window significantly limits the amount of air and heat loss from a room. Architects plan for these differences when inputting the size and selection of HVAC units to be used for an area. Windows with good insulating value require smaller HVAC units; those with poor insulating value require larger units. Each variable affects the utility cost as well.

Window styles can also influence price greatly. Windows with built-in glass partitions are normally much more expensive than similar windows that are solid with fake or trim window panel separations. Likewise, the solid windows normally insulate better than the ones with built- in metal or wood partitions because each of the seal points of the glass represents another point where air and heat can eventually escape.

Again, each difference represents a cost variable that the health care organization must plan for in every expansion project. Failure to plan for these issues is likely to result in lost revenue and a poor-performing venture. Likewise, planning for these differences ensures that construction cost variables work for the organization and help to meet everyone's expectations for financial performance, now and in the long run.

EQUIPMENT PLANNING ISSUES

The health care industry uses some of the most expensive equipment imaginable as compared to other service industries. Equipment costs can easily bankrupt an otherwise solid expansion project if not managed wisely and closely. Perhaps no other area has the potential for waste, negligence, and abuse that this one does. Equipment planning is also the area with the most budget breakers. Usually these unforeseens represent equipment that is common to projects but often left out of the initial assessment. Also, equipment planners sometimes take into account the major items of equipment but neglect required options, software, connections, installation charges, shipping, training, and service support.

Equipment costs can easily bankrupt an otherwise solid expansion project if not managed wisely and closely.

The best way to prevent this type of problem is to create an equipment planning worksheet or spreadsheet divided according to the individual project areas or rooms. Sometimes it is helpful to have one worksheet cover each type of equipment needed and then compare the worksheets to be sure nothing of importance has been left out. For instance, a typical project may have a furniture item checklist, a small-equipment checklist, and a major-item checklist. Here are issues frequently overlooked in planning the equipment budget for an expansion project:

Commonly Overlooked Equipment Issues

Surgical lights
Soap and towel dispensers
Temporary storage and power
Televisions, media devices
Addressographs
File drawers, storage bins
Storage shelves and cabinets
Exam and procedure tables
Equipment training costs

Electronic thermometers
Equipment interfaces
IV poles, pumps, stands
Bedside tables and chairs
Fax and copy machines
Window treatments
Common-area furniture
Service contracts
Equipment supplies
Wall-mounted equipment

Installation charges
Extra battery packs
Portable exam lights
Telephone systems and jacks
Computer workstations
Entrance-and-exit signs
Power cords and adapters
"Required option" packages

Negotiations for equipment purchases are a critical part of the budget control process as well. Unfortunately, equipment installed as part of an expansion project is frequently purchased at list price or higher, because the budget is often set up using product catalogues or standard vendor quotes. In many cases, vendor selection decisions are made in a committee meeting without the benefit of a competitive bidding environment. Preliminary equipment selection should be made as early as possible so that potential vendors can be brought into a competitive bidding process that eliminates excess costs from the equipment selection process.

Most health care organizations could save upwards of 25 percent or more on equipment purchases if completed under a competitive arrangement. Further, better financial concessions can generally be gained if the majority of equipment needs are met by one or two vendors under a bundled equipment purchase.

Equipment planning should also involve fixing responsibility for equipment delivery, storage, accountability, and installation. This is especially critical when new construction is being considered in which a contractor may be responsible for staging equipment installations in accordance with subcontractor schedules. If equipment is purchased from the vendor without fixing responsibility on these items, then it is possible that the equipment could arrive and be signed for by someone who is not familiar with it (a construction worker or the wrong subcontractor). Worse, equipment that arrives prematurely on site may end up damaged before installation. The responsibility for damage probably falls on the health care organization if these issues are not clearly spelled out in the purchase agreement. It is better to fix the responsibility for shipment and timing on the contractor and supplier so that they are forced to work together to alleviate any inconsistencies in responsibility and handling.

Project expansion objectives and financial performance goals can sometimes be met by substituting new equipment with used or refurbished equipment. This can be an effective way to align new service goals with the reality of restricted reimbursement. Used equipment can ordinarily be found that is in nearly new condition. Indeed, many health care organizations nationally have been closing and selling off equipment assets. In many cases, this equipment can be purchased at a fraction of the cost of the new counterparts. Additionally, a health care organization may have extra equipment in departments and clinics that is idle most of the time. This equipment can be repositioned into new expansion areas to offset equipment purchase costs.

SUMMARY

Projects must be carefully managed to keep within original budget constraints, especially since it is commonplace for organizations to go over budget. Generally, it is the incremental costs associated with project completion that gradually push costs beyond their initial estimates. Project partners should work together as watchdogs, making careful initial preparations to avoid unnecessary changes once the project is being implemented, and making recommendations throughout the project to reduce costs and increase overall project efficiency.

The cost of construction is especially high for the health care industry. This may be justifiable for construction of complicated, medically necessary hospital projects. However, it is important to make certain that this construction rate is not being charged when regular and nonspecialty construction projects are under consideration. Research into the going construction rates per square foot, as well as sensitivity to material and supply costs, positively affects the overall project cost.

Additional areas for consideration of cost-effectiveness include analyzing the highest and best use of space as it relates to the cost of construction. This is especially evident in older health care organizations in which the location of a new project may be contingent upon correcting past mistakes. Another area of cost containment is in planning for future growth during a project through installing the infrastructure that is necessary rather than spending unnecessarily for anticipated growth (which is in reality unknown).

It is likewise important to analyze whether an expansion should be located off site or on site. A variety of elements affect whether it is feasible, necessary, or prudent to locate certain projects on site. The cost of construction, regulations, and even patient demographics have an impact on the decision-making process.

Of major importance in any construction project is the variability of costs. Project managers should monitor every aspect of variable cost for utmost efficiency, including the cost of construction material and even the variability of labor owing to fluctuations in the construction industry. Understanding and communicating the importance of cost-effectiveness to the construction managers and then checking for compliance helps to keep variable costs down.

Equipment costs should also be planned for according to the best bid, rather than simply using list prices from manufacturers. This, as well as making certain that all related equipment add-ons are considered, allows greater accuracy in determining a project budget. Careful negotiation for the purchase of major equipment is critical, especially since most vendors have considerable profit margins built into their equipment costs.

QUESTIONS TO PONDER

1. Does your health care organization maintain adequate control over the project expansion process to ensure that budget control guidelines are met?

2. To what extent are projects managed within an overall project scope?

3. Are pro formas used to measure project completion goals? If so, to what extent have they been useful?

4. How much latitude do project managers and committee members have in exceeding project budget guidelines? What processes are in place to hold them accountable?

5. What percentage of project changes are made early in the project planning cycle? Do changes normally involve paper-oriented changes (that is, design and architectural drawings), or physical changes?

6. Is there a higher cost associated with changes made late in the project planning process? Why or why not?

7. Are contractors held accountable for supply and labor costs used toward project completion goals? If so, how are they made accountable?

8. What incentives are in place to focus project leaders on being aggressive in saving project implementation dollars? If in place, what tie is there from these incentives to quality outcomes?

9. What type of budget control tools are used by the project leaders to maintain quality and monitor ongoing costs and completion schedules? Are they effective?

10. Are project costs periodically checked against other industry costs? If not, why not?

11. To what degree does your organization consider the highest and best use for medical real estate? What happens if there are conflicts among interested parties?

12. Is it possible to adequately allow for future growth without building for it? How (or why not)?

13. Does the organization routinely consider the differences between on-site and off-site costs in considering new expansion projects?

14. To what extent do construction cost variables affect overall project costs? What can be done to lower these costs?

15. Is equipment planning executed as a strategic part of the project expansion process? If not, why not?

16. How early are equipment vendors brought into the equipment planning process? Does this timing result in a more competitive bidding process? If not, why not?

17. Who is normally responsible for aligning equipment delivery and installation requirements with contractor implementation timetables? Is the current method effective in fixing responsibility on the contractor and supplier?

CHAPTER 12

Reimbursement and the Business Office

Functions for Success

T he typical business office of a health care organization today is functioning at only a nominal level. This is true despite the incredible need for this office to work at cutting-edge caliber to assist the organization in remaining viable and profitable. A complete realignment of the importance of this department needs to be embraced, including a commitment to fund, equip, and train those functioning in business roles. This commitment is especially important regarding issues of health care reimbursement. Within a given health care organization, many areas of inefficiency can be found. In recent years, the business office has had the additional task of understanding and adequately dealing with complicated reimbursement issues. Unfortunately, most business offices have been sorely undertrained and understaffed in dealing effectively with reimbursement science. This has naturally caused a large problem in the area of receivables, adding to the burden most health care organizations are experiencing in their bottom line.

This chapter encourages health care providers to reexamine the important role of the business office; it suggests ways to move the organization toward greater revenue by properly using this important organizational function. This is a total change of thinking for people who have in the past cut personnel and other funding needs in the business office. As with other areas, the business office may appear to be one with "unnecessary fat," but as this chapter points out, the business office can be a vital channel for a successful revenue stream.

TIME FOR A PARADIGM SHIFT

Never before in the history of health care has the reimbursement climate been more confusing than it is now. Contract language, service restrictions, and regulatory gray areas abound within the industry, and health care providers are finding it more and more difficult to accurately predict cash flows stemming from patient-care services. This complex landscape of unprecedented lost revenues has created a political and business climate that often controls costs by restricting both services and operational decisions. This in turn has produced an increasingly time-consuming, bureaucratic decision-making process that is affecting the quality and profitability of health care in the United States.

As providers continue to lose money in this unpredictable climate, administrators attempt to control costs by cutting staff, training, and equipment purchases. These reductions further fuel the downward spiral of the organization as additional reductions contribute to stagnated growth, eroding market share, lost revenue, and poor consumer confidence. Many organizations are caught in a vicious cycle of declining revenue and rising patient care cost, but they are unable to correctly deal with the problems that caused it.

It is now time for health care organizations to embrace a significant paradigm shift. Conceptually, what has been happening throughout the industry is that providers are primarily operating from a defensive posture instead of an offensive one. This must change if the organizations ever hope to regain predictable profit margins and opportunities for long-term growth. Fortunately, many of the profit strategies needed to restore growth can be exercised through reinventing the business office practices of the health care organization.

Predictable profit margins and sustainable growth are achievable if the business office functions as a strategic operating unit, incorporating the best training, performance standards, reimbursement coordination, and research

188   Streamlining Health Care Operations

available. The environment of reimbursement for the health care industry is complex, but certainly not any more so than other highly competitive business environments. The conditions found in importing and exporting, discount retailing, or the commodities market are also highly complicated, yet predictable cash flows are achieved through strategic application of growth and profit retention strategies.

Conceptually, what has been happening throughout the industry is that providers are primarily operating from a defensive posture instead of an offensive one.

The discount retail market, for example, is highly competitive. Profit margins often hinge on the negotiating skills and market knowledge of the buyers who travel the globe looking for new and more cost-effective products. The Wal-Marts of this world could not remain financially viable if they did not invest deeply in the training and skill-building activities needed by these buyers. Health care business office personnel should likewise be trained to the utmost ability to extract the highest profit margins from existing and emerging services. Contracts should be negotiated, coordinated, and executed with maximum involvement from the contract negotiation team, the providers of care, and the business office staff.

Unfortunately, in many health care organizations, there is little or no coordination among business office personnel, the contracting office, regulatory bodies, and the third-party payer groups. This lack of coordination, training, and expertise results in misunderstanding, poor contract performance, and lost revenue. The problem is made worse when administrators arbitrarily cut business office staff to reduce operating costs. Staff reduction usually affects both the quality and the quantity of the reimbursements to be received thereafter. This is especially true with difficult contracts, those that contain hoops and restrictions and that often become poor-performing contracts after experienced personnel are cut from the staff or given more responsibilities to make up for cuts elsewhere.

In many health care organizations, there is little or no coordination among business office personnel, the contracting office, regulatory bodies, and the third-party payer groups.

To make matters worse, ambiguous contract language and restrictive reimbursement channels are becoming the norm for both private and government-insured policies. Both sides are seemingly engaged in a war with the provider community to contractually limit the rising costs of health care. This restrictive climate adds cost to the health care community because providers must spend many additional hours collecting reimbursement revenues from the existing patient base. This additional work creates a reduction in the productive payback of the services rendered and in the percentage of reimbursement actually realized.

Finally, many health care organizations are experiencing a drastic rise in bad-debt accounts, which is linked to both the complicated nature of the reimbursement climate and the poor financial performance of the industry. Avenues for reimbursement are often so confusing that organizations

Avenues for reimbursement are often so confusing that organizations neglect to pursue revenue streams for procedures that are routinely conducted by the provider communities.

neglect to pursue revenue streams for procedures that are routinely conducted by the provider communities. In some cases, these lost revenues are a direct result of misinformation about how to recover underpayment or how to conduct an audit activity relating to a contractual payment. Additionally, many organizations bury the responsibility for these activities in operations mixing the accounting office and the business office. In other words, responsibility is not clearly fixed and departmental lines become barriers to the most effective collection and audit control practices.

In a letter to the author, Richard C. Muhlhauser, the president of Profit Line, a national managed care audit and recovery firm, offered an industry perspective* from his organization's experience with helping health care providers recover lost revenues:

Industry Perspective

Our audits have indicated that a 5 percent net underpayment factor is average; 90 percent of our clients have had actual experience ranging from 3 to 7 percent in net underpayments.

Here are the main reasons 100 percent accuracy is rarely achieved:

- Properly trained internal auditors are not assigned to exclusively audit all managed care payments and recover all underpayments. When qualified internal auditors are assigned, many times they are given other unrelated projects to perform simultaneously, or are pulled off the project altogether.
- If management chooses to employ an expected reimbursement system, many times the system cannot correctly calculate all of the payment arrangements called for in a hospital's managed care contracts. Other times the system may not be properly implemented, maintained, or used. If the patient accounting staff cannot rely on the expected reimbursement data 100 percent of the time, errors are inevitable.
- Patient account representatives, collectors, and cashiers are not properly informed about all contract payment terms for the various managed care agreements in force. This can cause erroneous contractual adjustments. Sometimes new payment terms are not transmitted from the contracting department to the patient accounting department on a timely basis, and when the data is

* Excerpt from letter dated Dec. 8, 1999. Used with permission. Profit Line, 95 Argonaut, Ste. 5, Aliso Viejo, CA 92656-1487.

finally received, an effort is not made to correct previous under-payments.

- Staff turnover is unavoidable and usually causes payment errors to go undetected for some period of time.
- Sometimes there are misunderstandings between the patient accounting department, the contracting department, and the payer as to particular contract payment terms. Months can elapse before the parties reach agreement and past payment errors may never be corrected.
- Many times hospital personnel understand how a particular claim should have been paid, but when challenged by a misinformed payer, the underpayment error is written off without further investigation.

CASH VALUE VERSUS PROCEDURE VALUE

In today's environment of heavily discounted managed care and capitated payment, it is critical that the health care organization fully understand its reimbursement dollars. Although this statement may seem trite, evidence of revenue losses abounds within the industry. This fact alone strongly suggests that many providers are counting on funding streams that never fully materialize. This is especially true with reimbursement trends stemming from new and emerging patient-treatment procedures.

What happens in many instances is that the organization bases strategic decisions on the procedure value of patient-care services instead of using the actual net cash value rate that is actually realized from the mix of payer groups that support the organization's customers. In most instances, procedure value is significantly different from cash value. Net cash values are often as low as twenty-nine cents on the dollar. Organizations usually get into trouble with poor reimbursement trends when pro formas for emerging or changing services are calculated using figures reflecting standard reimbursement that are supplied by vendors or other uninformed parties.

The health care organization must correctly align actual reimbursement trends with treatment paths that fit within the strategic objectives. Health care services are only sustainable to the degree that market rates reinforce customer usage. Service reimbursement loss leaders should be analyzed for elimination, contract rate renegotiation, or outsourcing. Patient-revenue loss procedures that are deemed

Health care services are only sustainable to the degree that market rates reinforce customer usage.

essential but cannot be realigned, eliminated, or improved should be critically assessed for their contribution to customer satisfaction, regulatory compliance, or charity treatment goals.

Charity provision goals can often be reconfigured to include a degree of cost reduction that is borne by the primary care provider (donated supplies or physician services, or similar negotiated reductions in service cost). This process often serves to flush out costs that are unnecessary because it forces everyone involved to agree to bear their own responsibility for charity care. Unfortunately, many participants are only willing to provide charity care if the total cost is assumed by the health care organization. Even so, this process can reveal opportunities to do away with charity programs that cannot be adequately supported by the organization.

TEST OUTCOMES AGAINST "RAW" NET INCOME

Patient billing and business office practices are complicated, and net revenue returns are extremely variable. Differences in performance among billing specialists, collection representatives, and other key business employees can translate into significant lost annual dollars for a health care organization. Additionally, automated assistance programs can be just as variable, resulting in huge differences in reimbursement trends even among similar payer mixes.

The health care organization should closely monitor the differences between staff and machines, and be prepared to immediately modify training or utilization tools as needed to stay ahead of problems within the business office. For example, a change in computer software is likely to trigger a decrease in effective collection of accounts for some period of time. This is true regarding both systems use and employee training. Likewise, changes in employee job functions, seasonal loads, new employee hires, or similar factors can also significantly affect the quality of reimbursement received.

Unfortunately, mistakes made in the business office do not get better with time. If left undetected and unresolved, they usually translate into lost revenue that may never be recovered. This is especially true of contractual agreements that are time-sensitive, where the trend in reimbursement amount is downward in proportion to the age of the account.

It is a good idea to bring in an external auditing team from time to time to test the validity of internal controls and programs. External personnel can usually discern trends or soft spots in the daily business operations that may be missed by in-house personnel. Additionally, sometimes external resources can provide a more cost-effective augmentation to the existing structure because they can be brought in for a short period of time and used as needed in lieu of hiring a large, permanent staff.

ALIGN FUNCTIONS FOR STRATEGIC GROWTH

"Every city or household divided against itself will not stand" (NIV version, Matthew 12:25). These words of Jesus still ring true today—even within a health care organization. The reality is that many organizations are constantly struggling to become profitable or remain so while dragging a chain of archaic business practices that cannot be sustained in the long run. The medical industry is especially complex in the realm of reimbursement science. A combined front is needed that pulls the best practices, expertise, and resources together to combat the profit-robbing methods of decades gone by. Organizations that want to remain profitable must change tactics to survive in today's highly competitive marketplace.

One key survival strategy needed today is alignment of all the business office functions to achieve sustainable growth and profitability. Most organizations have done little in the last decade to change their basic business office operations to meet the environmental changes. Business office operations remain virtually unchanged despite significant reimbursement changes within the industry. In many organizations, additional personnel and functions have been added to the operational climate, but they have not been integrated into daily business activities. Many of these functions and personnel have become independent contributors to the whole process instead of being an integral part of a changing business operation.

How can a health care provider maximize profits and remain financially viable when internal processes and departmental barriers exist that contradict one another?

For this to change, health care executives and administrators must find creative ways to align all of these duties in one focused operation. This can be done by team process, service realignment, reengineering efforts, or any number of acceptable methods, as long as the end result is a united workforce that is moving forward toward the same goal of profitability and sustainable growth.

Business office operations remain virtually unchanged despite significant reimbursement changes within the industry.

LEAD THE WAY IN REIMBURSEMENT TRAINING

Navigating through the waters of financial viability in health care today requires thorough knowledge of reimbursement science. It is no longer true that a service rendered is a service repaid. Many organizations are struggling to survive because they are giving away patient care services and cannot afford to do so. These unintended charities exist on the basis of misunderstanding and ignorance of reimbursement finance, cost-avoidance legislation, and related strategies on the part of both government and private payers. Regardless of the origin, codes, contracts, and compliance languages exist to curtail runaway health care costs. Some work well, while others serve only as frustrating barriers to both the provider community and the patient or customer.

Again, regardless of the origin, these control methods will exist in the health care arena for the foreseeable future. Therefore, it is vital that health care organizations fully understand the field of reimbursement and extract the most benefit allowable from this restrictive climate. The truth is that health care costs are out of control, and the industry needs to do something about it. Meanwhile, organizations should concentrate on a twofold effort: equip their personnel to be the subject matter experts in reimbursement science, and simultaneously work on projects that help to alleviate the unnecessary costs present throughout the industry.

To this end, health care organizations should lead the way in reimbursement training. Administrators need to spend resources to adequately train and equip the business office and related personnel to become the subject matter experts in their fields. In the same vein, technology, software, and other common business enablers must be incorporated throughout the health care industry to keep up with the growing information boom that is sweeping every other industry. Organizations need to learn how to integrate technologies and information flows from all related infrastructures. Additionally, business office personnel should lead the way in learning how to use these modern-day tools so that the health care industry remains atop every new wave of change.

Organizations need to learn how to integrate technologies and information flows from all related infrastructures.

Many personnel are now using archaic business practices and home-grown software packages. They continue to fall further behind in their knowledge of best-practice initiatives and often are forced to use outdated equipment rather than modern technology and applications readily available in the marketplace.

EXCEL AT PREREGISTRATION

Preregistration is by far the most important function carried out by the business office staff. Preregistered patients are happier and better-paying customers. This is so for a number of reasons. First, preregistration significantly reduces the average wait time for customers to be seen once they enter the establishment. Second, financial issues can be dealt with prior to their becoming a problem for the provider, the health care organization, or the responsible payer. Third, pre-registered patients are far more likely to feel good about the experience they

Preregistration is good for everyone (except those who have no intention of paying for their medical bills).

receive at the health care organization, thus reinforcing the probability that the referring physician or plan will continue to do business with the health care provider. In fact, preregistration is good for everyone (except those who have no intention of paying for their medical bills). Even in these cases, it is far better to know about potential nonpaid claims in the beginning than after treatment has already been rendered.

Take as an example patients wanting to be treated at a particular medical facility that is not part of their primary care network of providers. In many cases, there is no justifiable reason for the patient to prefer one facility to another. From a financial perspective, the patient has a third-party insurance program that pays for the treatment at its own facilities, but switching to a provider from another network may invalidate the third-party payer's responsibility for paying for the service (especially in a case involving nonemergency treatment).

In a case of preregistration, the health care provider can arrange with the third-party provider for an exception to the normal authorizations to pay. If this is not possible, then an equitable agreement can be reached to allow the individual to use either cash or credit to pay for the services that are not covered by the primary plan. Finally, if the patient/customer is not willing to pay for the care separately, he or she is likely to be willing to return to the institution that has responsibility for primary care. This is especially true in cases where the decision is based on preference and not concern.

Although this example highlights some of the extreme benefits of preregistration, most of the value gained by the health care organization is seen in the normal day-to-day transactions that keep potential problems from becoming major ones for both the institution and the customer. Preregistration information obtained from customers usually consists of basic demographic data, such as type and extent of insurance; home and employer contact information; clinical background; physician or provider data; and the date, location, and timing of the service needed. Any of these information requirements can present problems in procedure authorization, scheduling, or reimbursement and payment. Problems encountered in preregistration are usually easier to solve than those arising after the patient has already arrived at the health care organization.

CREATE AN AUDIT TRAIL FOR SUCCESS

Some of the worst financial problems facing business office personnel concern loss of critical patient data that affect patient billing. Lost or missing patient records, authorizations, physician or provider orders, lab or procedure requests, and similar discrepancies can upset collection of full payment for treatment rendered to patients. Records that are lost after a correct initial billing can still pose problems for the organization if they are requested for audit by a third-party auditor wanting to verify proper billing in accordance with contract, legislative, or other agreement terms.

Maintaining an effective audit trail is a must for any organization wanting to maximize profit potential. Haphazard processes and procedures lead to underpayment trends, which can significantly undermine the overall viability of the health care organization. Medical record storage and retrieval operations, handling procedures, record update and posting processes, and issues of timeliness and accuracy all contribute immeasurably to the overall ability of business office personnel to secure proper payment for services rendered. The problem is that these vital inputs and audit trail efficiencies are dependent on the quality of care delivered throughout the health care system.

Maintaining an effective audit trail is a must for any organization wanting to maximize profit potential.

To ensure success, process and procedure auditing functions must be carefully orchestrated so that cause and effect issues are clearly identified, measured, and corrected. Electronic inputs should be embraced for both patient records and the associated billing and accounting processes. Finally, even physician and other provider inputs should be analyzed and tracked to ensure timely and accurate delivery of information required to carry out billing.

SUMMARY

Changes in reimbursement methods in the last several years have drastically altered the effectiveness of the typical health care business office. Profits and growth have seen adverse impact as a result, and many organizational leaders have not been able to make the necessary changes to counter this problem. Because of this, it is now necessary for business office leaders to embrace a new way of thinking—one that insists on people becoming subject matter experts on reimbursement science. This new approach helps to position the organization to battle the complicated reimbursement climate more effectively, thus augmenting the overall viability of the organization. To accomplish this, business office personnel must be trained and given the appropriate equipment and other resources to meet this challenging task.

It is also of utmost importance that the organization align reimbursement trends with treatment paths that fit within its strategic objectives. Market rates must reinforce customer usage.

Internal and external auditing can prove beneficial in keeping track of true performance levels within the business office. Varying skill sets among employees should be analyzed and training implemented when and where necessary. Systems and equipment and their usage should be monitored for effectiveness.

Also crucial is the degree to which internal departments and personnel coordinate their various functions to further, rather than contradict, the goals of the organization. Business office personnel should be fully aware of the strategic goals of growth and profitability and be brought into the process as integral players. Creating a united workforce takes some planning and demands change within an organization. Methodologies such as team process and reengineering are useful in reaching these goals.

Patient preregistration is a key to sustaining consistent customer payment. Focusing on preregistration can significantly improve the financial health of practically any health care organization, since this procedure increases customer satisfaction and provides greater assurance of reimbursement.

Record keeping and other critical patient data tracking are important to proper and efficient procedures within the business office. If they are inadequate, the result is curtailment of proper patient billing. Creating an audit trail is vital to an organization wishing to remain viable and healthy, as the trail attends to medical record storage, retrieval, handling procedures, updating, and timeliness and accuracy.

QUESTIONS TO PONDER

1. To what extent has your organization been operating from a defensive, not an offensive, posture regarding business office operations? What can be done to improve the organization's performance?

2. Is the business office operating as a strategic operating unit? If not, why not?

3. How are the profit retention problems facing the health care industry like those faced in the commodity markets, the discount retail industry, and the import-export business?

4. How much coordination exists among business office personnel, the contracting office, and the third-party payer groups representing your health care organization? Can it be improved? How (or why not)?

5. Has staff been cut as an attempt to restore profitability in your organization? If so, have the cuts been effective?

6. To what extent have equipment purchase delays occurred? Has this affected market growth or customer satisfaction?

7. Are business office personnel highly trained in reimbursement issues? Does this education and training extend to most of the support staff? If not, why not?

8. Do barriers exist within your organization between the business office staff and the accounting department? How about other related areas? What is being done to improve relations and remove barriers?

9. How reflective of your organization was the industry perspective of underpayment problems found in health care organizations nationally? Based on these percentages, what dollar figure is probably attributed to lost revenue for your organization?

10. Is procedure value or net cash value used to make decisions regarding new or existing patient treatment paths?

11. To what degree are business office personnel and practices measured to determine the quality of outcomes associated with procedures for patient-treatment billing?

12. How up-to-date is the business office in terms of new technology and procedures?

13. Are all business office functions aligned correctly within your organization? Does this include specialty knowledge bases such as nurse auditors, information system personnel, and contract negotiators?

14. What percentage of your organization's admissions are preregistered? Can this be improved? If not, why not?

15. How strong an audit trail does your organization maintain with items billable to patients? Is it checked frequently? To what extent are personnel trained and kept up-to-date on changes in billing issues?

CHAPTER 13

Consultants

Less Is More

By and large, consultants are an expensive and often unnecessary expense for the health care organization. Frustration with current operations and lost revenue are the reasons most frequently given for engaging consultants, but doing so seems to lead just as often to more frustration and lost revenue—with added problems of employee disgruntlement and few real benefits realized. This is mostly due to failure to tie consultancy groups to tangible, guaranteed benefits from the work that they do. On the other hand, consultants who are tied to deliverables are frequently very beneficial to an organization.

Many a health care organization hires a consultant and ignores the talent within its own ranks. This is a double whammy for the organization, because it often leads to employee frustration as they see consultants doing little more than observing what they already know and understand. If the organization can empower the available workforce to make good changes themselves, consultants can frequently be avoided altogether.

This chapter points out the problems and benefits associated with engaging a consultant and gives sound advice on ensuring that an organization (1) gets what it pays for, (2) avoids an unnecessary long-term consulting relationship, (3) manages consulting services adequately, and (4) uses in-house services whenever possible. Finally, niche consulting services are examined in light of the cost-effective nature of employing consultants in areas involving little or no financial risk for the health care organization.

EXHAUST INTERNAL RESOURCES FIRST

The field of consulting boasts some of the best and worst examples of business energy ever conceived. Probably no other industry can claim such a diverse history of climactic victory and worthless waste. A consultant can be the health care organization's most profitable partner or its most notorious robber. Such is the field of consulting. Nevertheless, consultants do play an important role in every industry, and they can be beneficial if used wisely and appropriately.

> *A consultant can be the health care organization's most profitable partner or its most notorious robber.*

The first standard of consideration for engaging consultants is to definitively assess whether they are needed at all. The initial look should be inward, to see if organizational personnel can be used to address the consulting and resolution needs. The organization may already have employees who are able to solve the issues once they are directed to do so. The problem is not usually one of ability so much as time and resources. Motivated and talented in-house personnel can accomplish great things when challenged to do so by both appointment and necessity.

The danger with using organizational personnel is that they are often given responsibility for projects without being given adequate resources to accomplish the mission. For instance, they may be tasked to solve an important problem but continue to be held accountable for all of their other duties and functions. This is one reason outside consultants sometimes appear better able to solve problems that have stifled internal personnel. Consultants typically are brought in for one project or concern at a time and are not saddled with the responsibility or expectation to accomplish anything other than what is contracted. This pinpointing atmosphere undoubtedly makes it easier for the outside consultant to deliver the requested results.

204

Training can also be an obstacle for insiders. This concept can be proven rather easily by examining the who, what, when, where, and why of consultants. Consultants are often hired because an organization lacks talent or expertise in an area that is needed to survive or grow in business. The lack of talent may actually reflect the organization's natural deficiency in adequately training its workforce. The problem may not be lack of talent at all, but rather lack of continuous training for talented people who are already in the organization.

This is especially true for skill sets that can be obtained from seminars, leading-edge training institutions, and other emerging business education and training suppliers. In cases such as this, an organization may pay outside consulting firms hundreds of times over for the cost of sending one or more employees to a progressive training session. To make matters

The danger with using organizational personnel is that they are often given responsibility for projects without being given adequate resources to accomplish the mission.

worse, once the consulting organization leaves, it generally takes most of the skill set knowledge along. The consultants frequently neglect to train the existing workforce adequately to sustain the improvements gained. Obviously, some consulting firms have a bias for additional work that prevents them from fully sharing all of their tools and training. Otherwise, many organizations would have no reason to ask them to return for follow-up business. On the other hand, an employee who has been trained in the latest skill sets probably is more motivated to continue working for the institution because the employer is meeting many of the individual's growth and development desires.

Consider the number of skilled employees who can be hired for the cost of a single $1 million consulting contract: twenty people could receive an average salary of $50,000 each for a full year and concentrate on any number of difficult projects. The question then becomes, What can twenty people accomplish in a year's time? Obviously a lot, if directed appropriately. Additionally, it is important to remember that outside consultants rarely work exclusively for one client at a time. Rather, they are expected to be key members of several projects simultaneously. An organization that hires twenty people to work exclusively on one project for an entire year probably gains much more than a contract orchestrated through a reputable consulting firm. Unfortunately, the organization may believe (erroneously) that its consultants are working around the clock on its project even when absent from the site. This is rarely the case.

It is also critical to remember where many of these consultants come from. As the saying goes, the only requirement for being a consultant is to be from out of town. This statement actually contains an element of truth, because consultants rarely have greater skill sets than those of the organization's own staff. Most executives have had experience with employees leaving their organization to go to work for a consulting firm. The ex-employee turned consultant is then reprogrammed by the consulting firm to sell his or her skill set to other health care organizations. Unfortunately, many consultants receive additional training only in marketing and selling skills, thence to return to the marketplace to solicit business from other health care organizations using the same essential base of skills that they had while engaged by their previous employer. This common business practice suggests that employers often hire consultants who are no more skilled than their own staff members.

OUTSOURCE IF BENEFITS ARE CLEARLY EVIDENT

Consulting relationships can certainly be advantageous to a health care organization if internal resources do not exist or cannot be easily built up to solve pressing business performance problems. Therein lies the key to establishing a healthy consulting relationship, one that is mutually beneficial. Consulting contracts should be established only if there is unmistakable evidence to support the benefits of partnering with an outside team of professionals.

There are a number of reasons consultants may be able to accomplish a mission better than in-house personnel. First, outsiders often bring a new perspective to an organization, one that just cannot be conjured up from within. There are many reasons this is true—often simply that people and organizations sometimes get into business habits that are archaic or harmful. In many cases, they cannot see the forest for the trees. A fresh perspective from an outside consulting firm may be all that is needed to bridge the gap between lethargic business practices and sustainable growth.

Organizational politics can play a role in dampening internal project completion goals as well. Organizations often act stereotypically and bureaucratically because certain relationships and power struggles exist that make it impossible to change ingrained operating habits. Outsiders can often overcome bias because they bring with them no hidden political agenda and no expectation to take over operations from insiders.

KNOW WHO AND WHAT YOU ARE GETTING

One of the dangers of hiring outside assistance from consulting firms is that the organization often does not get who or what it originally pays for. Consulting firms often hire highly credentialed individuals to impress clients, but they often do not put them to work in the day-to-day climate of the health care organization. Typically, the well-known and respected expert is primarily involved in bringing in new business to the consulting firm and rarely used to solve the problems associated with client contracts. Problem resolution usually falls to teams of underlings who may or may not have significant access to the subject matter expert.

For this reason, it is critical for a health care organization to fully

One of the dangers of hiring outside assistance from consulting firms is that the organization often does not get who or what it originally pays for.

understand what the nature and extent of involvement of these key personnel is likely to be after the contract is negotiated and signed. It is also important to have a clear understanding of the number of personnel who are assigned to the project, and whether they have conflicting duties that may divide their interests in getting the project implemented successfully. Issues of this type should be spelled out clearly in the contract, along with measurable performance objectives for the consulting team.

A poorly defined consulting contract can needlessly bankrupt a health care organization and ultimately cause more harm than good.

Well-defined roles, responsibilities, and expectations help to keep everyone targeted and accountable to deliver the expected results. Consulting contracts can be extremely beneficial to the health care organization if orchestrated properly and aligned appropriately (to the needs of the client). A poorly defined consulting contract can needlessly bankrupt a health care organization and ultimately cause more harm than good. The key is to make sure "outcomes" exceed "outgoes"! Clearly outlined contractual expectations help to ensure that the dollars spent on consulting efforts are far exceeded by the results achieved by the consulting agency.

MANAGE THE PROCESS TO ENSURE EXPECTED RESULTS

Consulting projects need to be managed just as efficiently as any other important operation. "Measure twice, cut once" is a common rule of the carpentry trade. This saying can be extended to the consulting world as well. Unfortunately, many consulting firms spend much of their effort winning the initial contract and frequently fail to follow through with the degree of expertise and professionalism espoused during the selling process. Health care organizations should therefore carefully manage both the terms and expectations of the contract and its execution. Frequent checks and reviews of critical time lines and deliverable expectations protect both sides from unmet goals and financial problems.

In this industry great care should be exercised concerning consultants, especially at a time when frustration and panic over lost revenue and inefficiency can drive an organization to make an unwise choice. Certainly the goal of any organization seeking to retain a consultant is to increase revenue or decrease expenses above and beyond whatever fee is negotiated for the service rendered.

Someone within the health care organization should be given overall responsibility for ensuring the ongoing success of the project. It is wise to have milestones and short-term deliverables spread throughout the term of the project so that progress can be measured and analyzed for quality and benefit. Critical events, or show stoppers, require the most diligence and watchful oversight and should involve more briefing than other aspects. Realistically speaking, projects that are checked and carefully managed remain top priorities for both the consulting organization and the health care organization.

Unfortunately, many consulting firms spend much of their effort winning the initial contract and frequently fail to follow through with the degree of expertise and professionalism espoused during the selling process.

AVOID LONG-TERM ENCUMBRANCES

A consulting firm and its consulting projects can easily become an organizational crutch that grows to be a standard operational budget item, much like any other operating arm. Usually this kind of encumbrance ends up costing the health care organization far more than it should. One of the best ways to prevent this from happening is to identify what aspects of the consulting relationship signal opportunity for replacement with internal employees or new hires. Employee education or training shortfalls should be analyzed early in the project to prepare for the eventual conclusion of the consulting relationship.

Do not expect the consulting firm to adequately plan for a professional retreat from the project at contract end. Many times consulting firms fully expect to renegotiate an extension or another job based on the relationships in place in the organization. Although it is true that some aspects of business are better handled by outsourcing, consulting activities are traditionally not set up as purely outsourced activities. Instead, consultants normally operate as primary advisers and short-term fix-it artists. This style of relationship is usually far more costly to maintain than a corresponding complete outsourcing effort. Mixed responsibilities often hide higher costs. This aspect of consulting projects should be thoroughly examined to be sure that valuable dollars are not wasted on long-term consulting relationships.

> *Do not expect the consulting firm to adequately plan for a professional retreat from the project at contract end.*

CONSIDER TRAIN-THE-TRAINER SERVICES

Costly consulting contracts can often be avoided by focusing on training efforts that enable employees to learn the skills necessary to fix their own organizational problems. This tactic is best employed through a train-the-trainer approach, in which key concepts are identified and key people prepared to direct and train the remaining organizational employees. One effective tactic for making this work is to use the eighty-twenty approach: identify the critical 20 percent of issues that are responsible for 80 percent of the problems, and focus training on these key issues. These in turn become the concepts that are learned throughout the organization. The noncritical 80 percent are then learned experientially as the project progresses.

Projects of this type are perfect for consulting relationships because the high-impact scope leads to the lowest contract cost for the highest possible benefit. The train-the-trainer approach also virtually eliminates the possibility of the consulting firm becoming a long-term encumbrance to the health care organization. This style of training is used successfully in the military, where training must often happen quickly and decisively to be of use in combat or emergency operations.

Costly consulting contracts can often be avoided by focusing on training efforts that enable employees to learn the skills necessary to fix their own organizational problems.

This technique can be used in a variety of ways. For instance, an organizational leader may find that a particular skill set can be readily learned by having everyone involved read a book on the subject. Further training can be extended through an intensive weekend retreat training project or similar scenario. Exercises of this type can be very effective at focusing on a particular philosophy of management or cost-cutting process. This train-the-trainer technique can further reinforce a learning process by sending key individuals to more extensive training.

NICHE CONSULTING

A number of specialty practices are emerging in the consulting field, targeted at problems that are truly niche market areas. This type of specialty often springs up as a result of inadequacy in broader education and training, normally filled by business colleges and other critical industry sustainment partners. Niche consulting groups often monopolize a particular area of expertise and may not share the information or expertise with others so as to retain a tight hold on the market for as long as possible. In any case, these specialty areas should be looked at very closely, in terms of growth trends and as an area of potential long-term outsourcing.

Sometimes niche markets are created to support temporary consulting activities that are known to be short-term in nature. For instance, many health care organizations engaged year 2000 (Y2K) consultants to handle their project remediation goals and be properly prepared for the transition into the new millennium. Now many organizations are turning to niche market consultants to set-up and run e-commerce opportunities for their businesses to make better use of the Internet market expansion capabilities.

Niche consultants can be very effective at highlighting and solving health care problems that might otherwise remain undetected or be too complicated for internal employees to address properly. For example, there are consultants who specialize in finding and resolving lost reimbursements. Fees are frequently tied to success at recovering them, so the organization benefits from the consultants' tangible success. This is certainly the safest and surest method for retaining consultants, and it obviously should be used to a much higher degree throughout the industry. Any time a consultant can be retained and tied to tangible monetary success, the approach should be carefully considered by the organization as an almost guaranteed benefit to the bottom line.

SUMMARY

Determining whether or not a consultant should be retained is a critical, and often costly, decision for any health care organization. At the outset, consultants can paint a very hopeful picture for the ailing organization. The promises, and the methods for accomplishing them, need to be carefully weighed prior to any commitment. Careful analysis of available in-house assets should be done before any consultant group is retained.

The costs associated with retaining a consultant are often more than those of hiring several competent and single-minded internal employees. This needs to be carefully analyzed, particularly if the added benefit requires the continuous presence of someone who understands the process. In such a case, an organization should be prepared to "permanently" retain the consultant, or be willing to hire and train an internal employee for the task.

Proper training at leading institutes should also be considered to keep the changes in-house as much as possible.

Caution should be exercised in retaining consultants so that the organization knows who will be doing the actual work. Subject matter experts who do not do the actual internal work frequently hold the job of selling client organizations on consulting. Assurances should be made that those conducting the day-to-day consultancy work are qualified themselves (above and beyond what is available using in-house expertise).

Hand in hand with the caution exercised at the outset of the contract should be continuous good management of the work as it progresses. Simply leaving consultants to do whatever their hands find is an almost certain guarantee of wasted time, energy, and money. The health care organization must closely monitor the project, as it would any in-house project that requires accountability and progress reports.

To avoid long-term encumbrances, it is wise to define the parameters and anticipated outcomes from the beginning. Processes should be in place that allow the consultant group to gradually transition out of the health care organization, particularly if special in-house training is required. Since the consultant only benefits from a prolonged stay within the organization, the health care organization needs to be cognizant of when a project reaches conclusion.

There are options other than retaining a consultant as well. The organization should exhaust its internal resources, and also consider train-the-trainer type services to keep things as internal as possible since this is generally the most cost-effective route and carries the most long-term benefit.

Outsourcing to consultants should be used if there are obvious advantages to doing so. This can be true in a number of cases, such as expert knowledge that would be cost-prohibitive for an organization to obtain other than through a consultant. Also, in cases in which internal politics makes it difficult to attain certain goals, a consultant can play a very important role in being an unbiased, external partner.

Finally, niche-type consultants who can tie their payment to deliverables pose the least risk and are often the most beneficial to an organization's bottom line. Careful analysis and contractual language should allow the organization to tie payment for services directly to an increase in revenue or a decrease in expenses.

QUESTIONS TO PONDER

1. Does your health care organization routinely recruit internally to fill critical project-related roles instead of automatically relying on outside consultants?

2. Is outsourcing clearly done on a need-only basis, or have some consulting activities been engaged unnecessarily? Why or why not?

3. Are organizational personnel given special training whenever skill sets are needed to fulfill emerging-project or special business opportunities?

4. What steps have been taken to ensure that consulting relationships truly reflect the needs of the health care organization?

5. Are consulting contracts negotiated in a way that ensures the organization is getting the level of consulting talent expected?

6. What methods or processes are in place to be sure responsibilities and expectations regarding consulting contract deliverables are achieved?

7. Does your organization assign someone to manage the consulting relationship? If so, has this practice proved beneficial? How (or why not)?

8. Are contracts negotiated to ensure that there is a good exit strategy for the consultants at the end of the contract term? What has been the historical experience of your health care organization after a consultant contract ended? Have the contracts been frequently renegotiated or extended?

9. To what extent have train-the-trainer services been used to maximize effective use of consulting services? If used, were they cost-effective?

10. How effectively have niche-type consultants been used within the organization? Will this change in the future? Why or why not?

CHAPTER 14

Special Concerns

Drive Out Waste

Every organization has pockets of waste and inefficiency that need to be eliminated or pruned to improve profitability and sustain growth. In an industry under intense pressure to cut costs and increase revenues, areas such as utilities, phone services, housekeeping, linen services, vending and contract negotiations, and even bureaucracy can contribute to or seriously take away from the success of the organization. This chapter pinpoints these and several other areas and suggests valuable methods for fixing these problems.

Much of the success of rebuilding a viable health care industry rests on the need for everyone to embrace a new paradigm of efficiency and cost consciousness that permeates every decision made. This ideal will come about only as leaders purpose to scrutinize every stone in the health care delivery edifice and to chip away at those that add no value.

UTILITY AND PHONE SERVICE COST

A health care organization can reduce annual operating costs significantly by taking advantage of the myriad market opportunities available to manage utility services efficiently. The utility industry is becoming more and more deregulated every day, and this environment of decreasing regulatory control is creating tough competition within the industry, which translates into less cost for everyone. Technological advances in electronics, computer systems, monitoring devices, and related equipment are helping everyone discover the best practices for maximizing the value of every energy and utility resource used.

Choices and opportunities abound for lowering utility costs. Nationally, many organizations are taking advantage of the new market conditions and are purchasing utility services from out-of-state providers instead of local utility companies. These practices are fueling regional wars on price reduction for every type of energy sold. Health care organizations are also finding that new operating systems, boilers, heating and air conditioning units, and monitoring devices can be bought and paid for out of current budget periods because the savings are astronomical compared to the cost of replacing antiquated systems. Many utility companies and third-party players are actually funding replacement of older systems to be able to continue providing business to health care institutions.

Today there are a number of energy management systems available in the marketplace that allow organizations to easily monitor and control the supply and delivery sides of utility usage. Additionally, many of these management systems can help the organization track and audit the supplier as well. As with any industry, mistakes in billing rates, performance measures, and unmanaged costs can translate into significant wasted dollars. Here are some of the utility issues that can be monitored and controlled to maximize revenue retention for the health care organization:

Utility Monitoring and Control Issues

Consumption rates	Humidity and climate effect	Thermal performance
Temperature variances	Energy efficiency	Comfort objectives
Trend and cost data	Load management	Sensor performance
Device proficiency	Flow and rate efficiency	Industry comparisons

Utility consumption should be tracked as a billing issue as well. Many health care organizations mistakenly assume that metered activities are correct and that suppliers rarely make mistakes. Unfortunately, there are a number of billing issues that can be incorrect, including the meter readings and consumption charging activities. For instance, organizations may be charged highly variable usage rates that are not consistent with either the contracted rate or those offered to other users. Likewise, some health care organizations are charged usage rates that include inappropriate tax charges. Many of these rates should be adjusted downward for applicable tax exemptions and use or size demographics. Additionally, some users qualify for unused utility buy-back credits for utility supply provided by in-house generators and similar sources. The next list shows typical issues that should be considered when auditing the billing invoices of major utility suppliers.

Energy and Utility Bill Auditing Issues

Tax rates	Billing rates and	Cost basis and
Number of meters	period	comparisons
and coverage	Contractual	Energy usage
Computation and	compliance	Penalties, terms,
billing errors	Verification, flow,	conditions
Billing cycle	usage	Variable-rate
Usage credits	Energy profile	pricing
Exemption clauses	Meter readings	

Good utility management often involves replacement of inefficient equipment, lighting, and monitoring and control systems. The truth is that cost reductions in this area normally include a well-rounded approach to eliminating waste in practically every arena of energy and utility usage. Many health care organizations have been involved in a number of programs to reduce operating costs and may find that these improvements have to be updated every five or six years to stay abreast of the latest energy-saving advances available. Each equipment and supply replacement or purchase decision should be balanced against the long-term cost of supplying utility power to the device. Many times, equipment manufacturers cut production costs by lowering the utility efficiency of equipment, thus passing on higher life-cycle costs to the health care organizations. These variables should be assessed as part of the total cost of equipment so that price concessions in the beginning do not end up costing more in the long run.

Many times, equipment manufacturers cut production costs by lowering the utility efficiency of equipment, thus passing on higher life-cycle costs to the health care organizations.

Phone service costs should be reviewed just as thoroughly as any other utility area. The telecommunications industry is even more deregulated than the other utility industries, and this climate of competition creates greater need for close scrutiny of costs related to phone service. Variability of cost is normal, and billing and rate discrepancies are extremely common within the entire industry. Likewise, phone services are also highly variable regarding the type of phone utility. For instance, cellular phone service rates are completely independent of line-service rates, yet the number and type of contractual agreements in place can affect each service. This is especially true for umbrella agreements where the same provider of cellular services supplies standard phone services. Even when contractual relationships exist, variation in billing rates, bundled services, repair rates, and other issues can be considerable. Therefore it is important for the health care organization to carefully manage the full scope of services provided and test the costs against those of other service providers. A number of variables should be examined in attempting to reduce the cost of phone services:

Phone Service Usage and Cost Variables

Local and long-distance rates	Bundled rates and packages	Incoming and outgoing rates
Extended service areas	Billing charges	Repair and service charges
	Line charges	

Cellular phone contracts	Regional or national contract	Call billing and timing change
Per-minute and per-second costs	Uptime guarantees Roaming charges	Value-added options
Tax exemptions and rates	Operator assistance rates	
Installation and hookup rates	Commercial and business rates	

HOUSEKEEPING

Like many other service areas within the health care organization, house-keeping services can greatly affect the overall operating costs and revenue-generating ability of the provider. For instance, the speed and quality of housekeeping services directly affect bed turnover rates. Additionally, infection and disease transfer rates are also driven by the quality of the cleaning and disinfecting process used by the housekeeping staff. Further, the cost of cleaning supplies and equipment can become excessive if not managed closely. Any and all of these issues, and more, can contribute to poor performance and cause the health care organization to lose ground financially.

Housekeeping managers and leaders should be challenged to proactively consider each and every area of operation in terms of its overall contribution to restoring revenue preservation or enhancing capability. Staff should be trained in the most expedient, efficient, and quality-conscious methods for delivering housekeeping services. Supplies and equipment, too, must be purchased in a manner consistent with the long-term goals of the institution to include purchasing methods favoring economies of scale, expertly negotiated contracts, and other procedures that minimize the costs of conducting business.

Additionally, housekeeping activities should be monitored and observed for opportunities to decrease the amount of time, energy, and personnel needed to restore cleanliness and use to functional areas. Reengineering studies, process improvement research, and other methods for improving daily operations should be used to the maximum extent possible to continuously improve the housekeeping function. Areas of weakness such as employee absenteeism or turnover should be looked at closely to find ways to lower the costs associated with initial training and long-term employee retention.

Health care organizations can learn a lot from other industry players as well, such as market leaders within the hotel and hospitality industry. Marriott International for one has become so proficient at managing cost and maintaining excellent quality that it exports and sells these practices to other industry participants. Marriott housekeeping procedures are legendary from the perspectives of efficiency and customer service. The truth is that hospital room turnover practices can be controlled to the same degree of timeliness, cost-effectiveness, and excellence as in any other industry.

SECURITY

The quality and consistency of security operations affects virtually every area of the health care environment. Health care organizations lose millions of dollars annually to theft and inattention. Unfortunately, equipment and supply losses are a common problem that involves both internal and external theft, organizational neglect, compassionate gifts to patients, and many other related costs that end up negatively affecting the bottom line of the organization.

Security issues are wide and deep. Every door, window, and opening in the health care structure is a potential avenue for loss. The security department or manager alone often handles the issues surrounding security, with little input or assistance from other organizational leaders. This needs to change if health care organizations are going to win the battle against losses in this arena. Security personnel normally have only limited ability to prevent the majority of losses. Much of what is needed in the way of prevention must be accomplished by systems, procedures, and oversight activities that have to be carried out at the individual department or unit level.

A comprehensive security program must include parking lot security, lighting plans, alarm systems, surveillance equipment, and an educational program fostering input and participation throughout the health care environment. Obviously, each of these costs must be weighed against the potential for loss that exists within each category of prevention. Some areas require more structure and support than others do. Certain key factors must be considered when establishing security measures and loss-prevention programs:

Loss-Prevention and Security-Consideration Measures
- Quantitative history of loss
- Climate of crime in immediate area
- Existing security systems currently in place
- Percentage of loss attributable to employee pilferage and gifts made to patients
- Education and participation level of organizational staff
- Organizational climate and policy for physician use of supplies
- Lighting, alarm, and surveillance environment
- Number and quality of professional security personnel
- Quality and support of local law enforcement
- Number, type, and use of exits
- Equipment monitoring procedures and technology

PHYSICAL PLANT EQUIPMENT

Infrastructure equipment within health care organizations is often the most neglected area of maintenance and upkeep. Boilers, chillers, generators, medical waste incinerators, and similar infrastructure equipment may be left out of annual budget allocations and capital-equipment replacement plans. Unfortunately, these oversights can end up costing an organization a lot. Typically, facility managers are pressured to hold off on replacing old equipment and thus end up wasting thousands of dollars in unreasonable repairs and upkeep that end up costing the health care organization much more in the long run. Many of these delayed replacements also affect the annual operating cost on the utility side because newer technologies outperform their older cousins and generally cost less to operate.

Much of the guesswork needed to make these decisions can be readily alleviated by comparing current and historical upkeep costs with projected costs of units currently available in the marketplace. Further, as mentioned earlier in the chapter, there are many businesses willing to sponsor the cost of replacing infrastructure equipment to benefit from the savings generated from lower utility costs. In many cases, a little research can actually net the health care organization a gain from these replacements instead of an operating loss.

ENVIRONMENTAL, WASTE, AND RECYCLABLES MANAGEMENT

There are literally hundreds of ways to save on environmental cost, waste management, and management of recyclables. Many of these related areas pose opportunities for cost reduction and revenue generation. One of the biggest waste areas for health care organizations is environmental and hazardous waste handling and control. Hazardous waste typically costs ten to fifteen times more to dispose of than normal waste. Despite this huge difference in cost, many health care organizations routinely mix normal trash with hazardous waste. Often labeled the "red-bag" problem, this practice actually can cost an organization a lot in lost revenue annually. Education and policing is the key to eliminating this problem. Employees at every level must be trained to guard against this profit-robbing practice.

Environmental waste can also be eliminated through reprocessing single-use medical devices and supplies. Although currently a controversial issue, many organizations have successfully reprocessed millions of devices and supplies, thus limiting the cost of repurchasing the items and the associated expense of disposing of them through the organization's hazardous waste collection program.

Health care organizations can turn other costs into profit avenues as well. For instance, many hospital receiving docks and departments handle literally hundreds of thousands of cardboard boxes and countless tons of shipping materials annually. Much of this waste is thrown away at significant cost instead of being recycled as a source of revenue. Putting these programs into place often entails nothing more than signing on with a contracting agent that supplies the cardboard bailing machine. Likewise, crates, pallets, paper, and plastic can all be recycled to produce revenue instead of cost.

LINEN DISTRIBUTION

Linen costs can be highly variable as well. A health care organization should always strive to quantify the cost per pound to process linen supplies and compare these costs among multiple suppliers and delivery or service options. Quantifying costs of linen distribution often reveals areas of weakness within the health care system's process, thus allowing simple changes to be made to lower total overall cost. For instance, linen is often delivered to numerous sites within one organization, and these contracted delivery prices are often much higher than that of having deliveries made to one central location and picked up or distributed by employees or staff.

Costs can also be excessive if poor quality linens are used. The cost of purchasing or replacing linens is often not factored into the cost-per-pound equation for linen services. This can be a big mistake, since frequent repurchase of basic linens can add significant cost to any program. Additionally, many health care organizations do not maintain stringent controls on the accountability of linens. Employees and staff often take linen products home for personal use. Left unguarded, these practices can quickly add large unbudgeted costs to the linen reprocessing practice.

Linen costs can also be significantly affected by the quality of the cleaning and reprocessing service used. Some companies use harsh techniques for cleaning and processing linen items, and these methods can translate into unnecessary additional costs for the health care organization because the life of the linen items is reduced. For example, one linen company may use processes and techniques that allow linen items to be processed through fifty washings before reaching the end of their useful life, while another may process the linens using less harsh methods resulting in seventy-five lifetime washes.

Linen costs can also be significantly affected by the quality of the cleaning and reprocessing service used.

Although most employees would not suspect themselves of adding significant cost to an organization with these seemingly little indiscretions, the truth is that a few pens per employee per year can add up to a lot of cost over time.

Obviously, differences such as these cost the organization significantly.

The manner in which linens are purchased can also affect overall cost. Linens should be purchased under bundled agreements covering several years' worth of need. Historical purchases should be analyzed for budget trends so contracts can be negotiated that cover the probable number of linens to be purchased in a given year. This avoids the high-cost technique of purchasing replacement linens at small-volume prices. High-volume buyers of linen goods should receive pricing that is reflective of the volume of linens purchased annually. Additionally, an organization should try to form volume-purchase agreements with other partners as well to maximize the buying power of everyone concerned.

OFFICE SUPPLIES

It is a shock to learn how many dollars are wasted annually on items such as pens, pencils, and paper. Although it would be hard to argue with the need for many of these purchases, much of what is purchased ends up going home with employees and staff. (The correlation of costs is most evident at certain times of the year, particularly just before a school term begins.) Although most employees would not suspect themselves of adding significant cost to an organization with these seemingly little indiscretions, the truth is that a few pens per employee per year can add up to a lot of cost over time. Organizations can combat this in a number of ways, among them education and sensitivity training, stricter supply controls, or even eliminating purchases of these supplies. In many cases, the problem can be reversed effectively by giving individual employees the responsibility for small-item supplies.

Office supplies can also represent excessive inventory holding costs. This is a common area of inefficiency within practically every industry, including health care. Sometimes true inventories are difficult to assess because office supplies can be hidden in many locations besides the typical supply closet; employee desks, file drawers, and overhead storage bins often contain numerous unused supplies that never get used, even by the employees themselves. The organization can test this reality quickly by challenging every staff member to bring into one central location every extra pen, pencil, notebook, and other common office supply that they can recover within their area. The results would shock most leaders. Equally distressing is the variability of cost. Pens, for example, can cost anywhere from twenty-five cents to several dollars each. It is truly incremental waste like this that causes organizations to slip into financial ruin.

Contracting with the right suppliers can also significantly lower office supply costs. Again, organizations often base purchase and supply decisions on day-to-day operations and needs instead of looking at these budget items as yearly repeat costs. Items such as pens and pencils are much more expensive by the box than by the case. Likewise, paper purchased by the pallet is much more cost-effective than the same paper purchased by the package or ream.

VENDING SERVICES

Vending services can be a large source of revenue for a health care organization, as well as a morale booster for employees and staff. Major vendor contracts often net organizations several hundred thousand dollars of revenue per year with no added employee or operational cost. Vendors typically install, service, repair, and load their machines themselves and maintain responsibility for all of the logistics associated with vending sales. Likewise, most machines now capture

Vendors typically install, service, repair, and load their machines themselves and maintain responsibility for all of the logistics associated with vending sales.

sales information electronically for easy verification by both the vendor and the institution.

Although many organizations believe that vending may hurt cafeteria sales, there is little evidence to suggest that vending services interfere with traditional restaurant sales revenues. The health care organization should carefully consider the real usage of cafeteria services and compare this against the probability of more frequent sales being generated by vending machines that are located close to employee and staff work areas.

MAIL AND COURIER COST

Many variables are found in mail and courier services within the health care industry. The truth is that organizations suffer from redundant services and missed opportunities for courier and mail service. Both types of inefficiency can create unnecessary cost for a health care organization. For instance, an organization that relies on courier services for shuttling radiology films between physician offices and imaging centers may actually be underusing courier services if radiologist reading time and patient throughput is negatively affected by the long lead times associated with batching courier services. The same is true of lab services. Sometimes cost reduction in courier activity translates into an operational cost increase in another area. These issues need to be carefully considered when analyzing the cost-effectiveness of programs and services.

Planning is essential when orchestrating the effectiveness of mail and courier services. Each delivery route, location, and use should be analyzed for its proper fit and alignment within the overall service provision of the health care organization.

On the other hand, the organization may also suffer from significant overlapping services. A courier or mail service deliverer may cross paths many times as an individual service provider makes frequent stops at locations that could easily be covered by another institutional courier. Sometimes courier services are used to the exclusion of common interoffice mail services, which could serve the routine purposes of the organization. Planning is essential when orchestrating the effectiveness of mail and courier services. Each delivery route, location, and use should be analyzed for its proper fit and alignment within the overall service provision of the health care organization. Additionally, organizations need to carefully consider the viability of courier services to ensure that proper balance is maintained between in-house and contracted services. A transportation study is frequently advisable to validate the overall cost-effectiveness of these programs for the health care organization.

PHYSICIAN AND OTHER PROFESSIONAL EDUCATION

Education and training costs for physicians and other professional staff can be extremely costly for an organization. Unfortunately, lack of training can be just as costly in terms of lost revenue, inefficient practices, and constantly degrading skill sets. Obviously, the organization needs to establish parameters of control so that an effective balance can be maintained between need and cost. Many health care organizations have no overall plan to control spending in this manner, except annual budget allocations. Although budget constraints are important, this approach alone is not effective in maximizing the value of this critical area of education. Budget controls often limit the revenue stream because new skills are not picked up as quickly as warranted by changing treatment paths or emerging opportunities in the marketplace.

Methods of education must be considered as well. Traditional methods such as attendance at special schools, clinics, or seminars are often overly time consuming and expensive. Valuable skills can frequently be picked up by means of cable television, video conferencing, interactive CD, teleconferencing, and similar methodologies. It can be less expensive to bring the trainer to the organization than to have a number of people travel to a training site.

Training partnerships should be established as well. Health care organizations need to actively engage business partners such as vendors, suppliers, and association affiliates in the education planning process. These activities can be completed by interested third parties at minimal cost to the health care organization. Although most health care leaders would argue that this is already being done within their organization, the truth is that most of this collaboration is accomplished without the proper oversight needed to effectively tie these educational assets to the overall goals of the organization. What is not managed is likely not very effective or beneficial to the long-term goals of the organization. In the same way, lack of oversight and management in this arena frequently spells redundancy and unnecessary duplication of educational efforts in other related areas.

MEDICAL RECORDS

Medical records, like many other forms of historical records, can quickly become mammoth beasts, eating away at organizational efficiency and productivity. Organizations have a tendency to create more files, paperwork trails, and records than necessary. Although much of medical record upkeep is regulated by law and cannot be readily changed, most health care organizations err on the side of keeping too many records as opposed to not enough. A visit to just about any medical storage facility quickly reveals hundreds of opportunities to reduce inventory holding costs and retrieval and filing expenses, and even prevent the potential for future lawsuits. There are a number of costs associated with keeping records longer than needed:

Common Medical Record Holding Costs

Warehouse leasing costs	Copy and production expenses	Management and staff
Shelves, racking	Record retrieval expenses	Storage boxes and containers
Fire safety		
Lawsuits	Courier services	Reporting costs

| Air conditioning and climate | Automation and computer costs | Labeling and bar coding |
| Microfilm, optical transfer | Pest control | |

Medical record storage also includes expensive components such as radiological films, cassettes, and other forms of patient records that grow out of the normal day-to-day business of the health care organization. These specialty areas can become excessive as well and usually represent even more holding costs than the traditional ones. To protect against these cumulative cost problems, organizations need to have a comprehensive plan for storage, upkeep, retrieval, and destruction of each component of medical record keeping. Legal counsel and medical record management professionals should be equally involved in deciding the correct policy, methodology, and timing of record destruction. This ensures that historical files are eliminated systematically throughout the year so that inventory-holding costs do not continue to grow over time.

Legal counsel and medical record management professionals should be equally involved in deciding the correct policy, methodology, and timing of record destruction.

CONTRACTS

It seems that more and more organizations are finding ways to outsource business issues to external partners. Usually these services or supply venues come in the form of contractual relationships, which tie organizational loyalties to a particular vendor or supplier for some length of time. Although contracts can be very effective in controlling costs, they can also be a source of increased cost if not negotiated or managed correctly. The health care organization should ensure that personnel involved in contract negotiations are adequately skilled to deal with these issues so that the maximum possible value is achieved in each contract entered into. This applies to every form of contract, whether physician or provider contracts, maintenance and service support agreements, or those involving purchased goods or services.

Contract negotiations must not be done by inexperienced personnel, as is commonly encountered in numerous departments within the typical health care organization. Individual departments have biases, which may cloud their effectiveness in negotiating for services. For instance, a clinical lab may be facing budget constraints, which may cause the director or manager to opt for an agreement that ties all future reagent purchases to a capital-equipment deal. This type of arrangement may end up costing the health care organization two or three times the cost of negotiating the deal separately in a competitive environment. Unfortunately, these contracts are often negotiated because the individual department may feel powerless to affect capital-equipment replacements in any other way. Individual managers and directors often do not possess the skills necessary to negotiate with professionals from the vendor community. These disadvantages in training and technique can spell tremendous waste for the health care organization.

Individual departments have biases, which may cloud their effectiveness in negotiating for services.

BUREAUCRATIC WASTE

Organizational bureaucracy probably accounts for more waste per incident than any other area. Slow decision-making processes cost health care organizations billions of dollars every year in lost revenues and uncontrolled waste. This needs to be changed if the health care industry ever expects to regain strong profit-generating capacity. Employee motivation, morale, and

creativity are greatly curtailed if decision-making processes are characterized by sluggish and despondent
behavior. Expedient execution of
good ideas creates cost-conscious
employees who are excited about continuing improvement-oriented exercises. Nothing motivates additional
wins more than frequent victories.

The difference between peak performance and mediocre performance rests on the ability to predictably execute good decisions in a timely fashion.

The health care organization must
search diligently for ways to cut deci-
sion-making processes to the absolute minimum. The key to making this
happen is to fix responsibility for every action on key individuals and measure their success by the quality of the execution and the time frame that it
takes to achieve it. Anyone can make a project work if given enough time and
resources. The difference between peak performance and mediocre performance rests on the ability to predictably execute good decisions in a timely
fashion. Leaders who excel at making good decisions quickly should be given
control, whereas those who only survive under decision-making processes
with long lead time should be encouraged to either change their behaviors or
go work for someone else.

SUMMARY

Health care organizations generally have pockets of waste and inefficiency
throughout the entire organization. Making large and sweeping changes
may be good and necessary, but it is in the little, often overlooked, areas that
incremental changes can be made that positively affect an organization.
Good health care leaders embrace rather than shun these pockets to maintain a highly efficient organization.

As utility and phone companies have become deregulated, greater cost
savings become a viable opportunity for the organization looking to shave
costs off these necessary and costly obligations. Careful management can spell

the difference between a mediocre program and a healthy, money-saving one. Choices include various suppliers as well as myriad options and packages.

Housekeeping is another health care necessity that can be easily over-looked as a contributor to the bottom line. However, excellence is often neglected in this function (which includes training, supply costs, employee absenteeism and turnover, and job efficiency). Looking to industry leaders, as in the hotel industry, can prove an excellent benchmark for this area.

Security systems, as well as an overall organizational standard against inappropriate behavior, should be closely scrutinized. A comprehensive security system should be far-reaching, thorough, and well managed. Particular emphasis should be placed on loss-prevention programs.

Physical plant equipment is often archaic and undermaintained. The product of many budget cuts, it is unfortunate that important facility equipment is often the last thing to be replaced. This is despite the fact that proper maintenance and life-cycle management could significantly improve the overall efficiency of the organization. Even a little research and action into this problem arena can prove beneficial and profitable.

Costs associated with managing general waste, environmental waste, and recyclables should be taken very seriously. This seemingly small pocket is one in which great strides are possible in cost saving and revenue generation. As with community waste recycling, it is important to lay the groundwork for a strong program. Employee awareness and participation can make a difference in the degree of compliance and efficiency. Simple measures such as signing up for a recycling program can mean the difference between paying for waste pickup or receiving revenue for participation in a recycling program.

Other areas that are frequently given only brief consideration include linen distribution, office supplies, and vending services. Each of these operations may seem negligible at first glance, but the outlay and lack of careful monitoring can spell tremendous costs or lost revenues. Linens and office supplies should be negotiated for in a large purchase contract, as opposed to the high-cost method of ordering and reordering at retail cost. The health care organization should be aware of revenue-friendly services such as vending, which can add significantly to the bottom line.

A great deal of time and energy is needlessly expended on mail and courier services. Rarely is there appropriate coordination to take full advantage of the schedules and efficiencies, which could be attained here. A transportation study can shed light on the overall effectiveness of these activities and prove to be very cost-effective.

Time and money goes prodigiously into the education and ongoing training necessary to keep physicians and other medical professionals updated in their skill sets. Although it is very important to keep up with the latest medical and industry knowledge, it is also important to carefully analyze the highest and best use of bringing the training to the organization. Being creative and looking for ways to be cost-effective can greatly benefit an organization in this common endeavor.

Proper management of medical records is another operation in which organizations rarely excel. It is essential to meet the legal standards, but it is also important to remain realistic and prudent in filing, maintaining, storing, and disposing of such records. Proper counsel in how to manage this area proves vital and effective.

Health care organizations must carefully attend to the abilities of managers who might undertake contractual agreements in the course of their daily business. Experts in contract negotiation should always be involved in any such commitments. This can greatly reduce organizational cost and increase the chances of overall organizational streamlining.

Finally, the area of bureaucratic waste is one that seems to plague most sizeable organizations. There are always those who tend to impede action on projects; in so doing they are actually a detriment to organizational efficiency. Creating an organization that exalts timeliness and expediency can be very difficult, but it is worth the effort.

QUESTIONS TO PONDER

1. How has utility deregulation affected operations within your health care organization? Have benefits translated into bottom-line improvements? How (or why not)?

2. To what extent is technology used to capture additional savings from utility usage? Is this process reviewed frequently?

3. Is someone within the organization tasked with the responsibility to validate utility billing issues? If so, does this include the meter-reading and consumption-charging practices of the utility company?

4. Does purchasing staff consider utility efficiency when considering total life-cycle cost for new equipment? If not, why not?

5. How often are phone service costs reviewed? Does this include comparison of costs associated with cellular phone contracts, repair rates, and other associated phone utility costs?

6. Are housekeeping functions analyzed for both efficiency and expedient service? What about the quality of services rendered?

7. To what extent are security issues dealt with from a preventive posture? What can be done to improve the effectiveness of these operations?

8. Has physical plant equipment replacement been delayed within your organization? If so, how has this affected operational costs in other areas such as utility management?

9. Is recycling used as a cost-reduction tool, or as a revenue-enhancing tool? Has your organization considered other opportunities for recycling, such as reprocessing of single-use medical instruments?

10. How effective is the organization's linen management program? Are employees and staff held accountable for missing or damaged linens? If not, why not?

11. Are linens purchased cost-effectively? What basis is used for arriving at annual budgeted amounts? Is this method effective at reducing costs?

12. Would an organizationwide collection of office supplies reveal hidden inventories? Does anyone track the total cost of the program annually? What can be done to reduce these costs?

13. Do office supply costs increase just prior to the new school year? If so, is this the only area of cost that rises in relation to common commu-

nity events? Are employees aware of the overall cost of practices such as these?

14. Does your organization benefit financially from vending services? How (or why not)?

15. Has a study ever been done of mail and courier cost to maximize effective use of these services?

16. To what degree are educational activities monitored and aligned with the overall goals of the organization? What can be done to improve this performance?

17. Are medical records managed appropriately? Does this include specific guidelines for timely destruction of older records?

18. Does your organization negotiate and manage contracts professionally?

19. In what way are department directors and managers involved in the contracting process? Is this effective? What can be done to improve the process?

20. Would outsiders consider the organizational climate bureaucratic or decisive in nature? How do employees and staff rate the quality and timeliness of the decision-making process? Can it be improved? How (or why not)?

RECOMMENDED READINGS

Boulton, R.E.S., Libert, B. D., and Samek, S. M. *Cracking the Value Code: How Successful Businesses Are Creating Wealth in the New Economy.* New York: Arthur Andersen/HarperBusiness, 2000.

Bramel, J., and Simchi-Levi, D. *The Logic of Logistics.* Springer Series in Operations Research. New York: Springer-Verlag, 1997.

Covey, S. R. *The Seven Habits of Highly Effective People.* New York: Simon & Schuster, 1989.

Hartley, R. F. *Marketing Mistakes.* New York: Wiley, 1989.

Herzlinger, R. *Market-Driven Health Care.* Reading, Mass.: Addison-Wesley, 1997.

Hill, N. *Napoleon Hill's Keys to Success: The Seventeen Principles of Personal Achievement.* (M. Sartwell, ed.). New York: Plume/Penguin Group, 1997.

Juran, J. M. *Juran on Quality by Design.* New York: Free Press, 1992.

Miller, J. B., with Brown, P. B. *The Corporate Coach.* New York: St. Martin's Press, 1993.

Peters, T. *Thriving on Chaos: Handbook for a Management Revolution.* New York: Knopf, 1988.

Sherman, V. C. *Raising Standards in American Health Care.* San Francisco: Jossey-Bass, 1999.

Shortell, S. M., and others. *Remaking Health Care in America: The Evolution of Organized Delivery Systems.* (2nd ed.). San Francisco: Jossey-Bass, 2000.

Walton, M. *The Deming Management Method.* New York: Perigee Books/Putnam, 1986.

INDEX

C

Cab companies, lessons from, 27–28
Calibration, 161
Capital expenditures, reducing, 40
Capitated payment, 192
Case-by-case purchasing, 91, 92
Cash flow predictions, difficulty in, 188
Cash incentives, uses of, 59, 72–73
Cause-capturing methods, skill in, need
    for, 43
Cellular phone service, 218
Census information, basing need on,
    130–131, 177
Change: actively seeking, 60–61; commu-
    nicating, 19–20; embracing, need for,
    1; employee resistance to, 18–19;
    industry resistance to, 3–4, 103; pres-
    sure to, 7; sabotaging, 18–19
Charity provisions, 193
Chat-room format, 58
Chemical reagent costs, 120, 230
Chrysler, 11, 87
Classified want ads, 71
Collection department staff, 44, 193. *See
    also* Bad debts; Business office opera-
    tions
Community marketing plan, 71
Comparative analysis, examples of using,
    44–45, 87–88, *97*
Compassionate gifts, 220
Compensation, 44, 68, 72–74
Competition: internal, 40; vendor,
    153–154, 183, 230
Configuration variability, 137
Construction and expansion projects. *See*
    Expansion projects
Construction industry regulations,
    172–173
Construction materials, 171–172
Consultants: attitude towards, 203; back-
    ground of, 56; skill sets of, 206
Consulting contracts, 208
Consulting services: assessing need for,
    204–207, 211–212; long-term use of,
    avoiding, 209–211; overview of,
    203–204; and project management,

208–209, 210; questions involving, 214;
    summary of, 212–214; understanding
    nature of, 207–208
Consumable supplies, 161
Contract negotiations: cost-plus basis for,
    5; as a special concern, 229–230; train-
    ing in, 95, 96. *See also specific types of
    contracts*
Contractors, dealing with, 171–173, 183
Cost and quality alignment. *See* Quality
    and cost alignment
Cost avoidance, benefit of, 90–91
Cost estimation, for expansion projects,
    170–171
Cost-cutting measures, current methods
    of, 2
Cost-effective quality health care. *See*
    Quality and low cost
Cost-plus basis, 2, 5
Courier and mail services, 226–227
Creative problem solving: and bureau-
    cracy, 231; emphasizing, 16–17; foster-
    ing, 54–62; overview of, 53; power of,
    lesson on, 17-18; questions involving,
    64–65; summary of, 62–63
Critical project events, oversight of, 209
Cross-training, 72
CT scanners, 136
Customer groups: defining and segment-
    ing, 23–25; internal, identifying, 77–78;
    mixed, addressing, 25–26
Customer scheduling: addressing, 26–27;
    lessons on, 27–28
Customer service, 33, 76–79
Customer surveys, 58
Customer-driven culture, creating,
    75–79

D

Daily interaction from leaders, 61–62
Damaged goods, 105–106, 183
Data collection procedures, skill in, need
    for, 42, 43. *See also* Statistical collection
    tools
Debts, bad. *See* Bad debts
Defective items, 41

Group purchasing, 98–99, 100, 154–155
Growth needs, addressing, 7–8
Growth projections, 177, 178

H

Habits, ingrained, 4, 207
Harvard University, 95–96
Hazardous waste, 222, 223
Health care costs and marketplace alignment, 7–8, 18
Health Care Financing Administration (HCFA), 116
Health care industry status, overview of, 1–8
Health care needs, rise in, 74
Health care services, value of, calculating, 192–193
Hiring interviews, improving, 71–72
Holding costs, 135–136, 225, 228
Holding layers, 2
Hopelessness, 3
Hospitality industry, learning from, 76, 220
Housekeeping services, 219–220
Human resource department, 71, 72, 73
Human resources: areas for improving, 67–79; importance of, 67; lessons on, 79; questions involving, 81–82; summary of, 80–81. *See also* Employee value
HVAC units, 181, 216

I

Independent service organizations (ISOs), 143, 145, 151
Inefficiencies, combating. *See* Creative problem solving
Inefficiencies, identifying: common areas for, 47–48; fact-finding methods for, 41–45
Inefficiency: effect of, 39; variables of, 41
Infection and disease transfer rates, 219
Information flows, integrating, 196–197
Information networks, 58
Information technology, 39; for the business office, 18, 193–194, 199; integrat-

ing, 196–197; for purchasing tracking, 97. *See also* Internet projection
Infrastructure: for expansion, 177; internal, rebuilding, 2–3
Ingrained habits, 207
Innovation, creating, 60–61
Inpatient service, construction for, 178
Insourcing versus outsourcing: for consulting needs, 204–207, 211–212; of resale responsibility, 147; for servicing needs, 145, 149–152
Installations, 183
Insurers. *See* Third-party payers
Interconnectivity, between departments, 30
Internal motivation: capturing, 73, 74; in customer service, 78; versus external motivation, 15
Internet, employee use of, 58
Internet projection: leader in, 7; and niche consulting, 212; optimizing, 29–30
Interviews. *See* Hiring interviews; Personal interviews
Inventory: availability of, 138–139; control of, 7, 103; holding costs of, 135-136, 225, 228; layers of, 2

J

Job applicants, screening, 71–72
Job performance, 10–11, 12–13, 193–194
Joint Commission on the Accreditation of Healthcare Organizations (JCAHO), 138

K

Koenig, D. P., 151

L

Layoffs, 2, 40, 75, 188; costs of, 9–12, *13*
Lease-or-buy scenarios, 146
Legal counsel, using, 229
Liability for damaged goods, 105, 106, 183
Life-cycle cost. *See* Total life-cycle cost
Linens, 223–224
Local Area Network (LAN) standards, 117
Local experts, using, 148–149
Loss-prevention, 221

Lost reimbursements. *See* Bad debts
Luxury building features, 178, 179

M

Mail and courier services, 226–227
Maintenance and repair issues. *See* Service, upkeep, and repair
Maintenance, preventive: emphasizing, 150, 159–161; leader in, 7
Managed care contracts, 189, 190, 191–192, 193, 194
Manufacturers, 87; linking directly to, 98–99; original, 143, 145, 150, 151. *See also* Vendors
Market-driven purchasing, 115–117
Marketing, 30–34; leader in, 7
Marketing department, role of, in image building, 70–71
Marketing-based pricing models, 83, 84–86, 87
Marketplace alignment, 7–8, 10, 11, 18
Marriott International, 220
Matthew 12:25 (NIV version), 194
McDonald's, 7
Medical equipment and supplies, dependence on, 88
Medical records, 199, 228–229
Medical technology. *See Technology entries*
Medicare, 116
Mergers and acquisitions, 12, 135
Microsoft, 11, 93
Mission, redefining, 11
Morale and motivation: factors affecting, 13–14, 73, 231; gathering information on, 68–70; impact of, 14–15; improving, 15–16, 54; lack of, 12–13; lesson on, 79
Muhlhauser, R. C., 191

N

National Health Care Logistics (NHCL), 103
Negotiations. *See* Contract negotiations
Neodyme Technologies, 151
Net cash value of services, understanding, 192–193
Niche consulting groups, 211–212

Nordstrom, 76–77
Nuclear cameras, *93*, 95, 101, 115
Nursing staff, training for, 75

O

Office supplies, 224–225
Off-site costs versus on-site costs, 178
Off-site interviews, 69
Operating hours, extending, 34, 158
Option packages, 116, 136–137
Organizational goals: aligning, with real needs, 55; centering, on customer service, 76–79; obstacles to, identifying, 54. *See also* Vision
Original equipment manufacturers (OEMs), 143, 145, 150, 151
Outpatient service, construction for, 178
Outreach, 33–34, 178
Outsourcing versus insourcing: for consulting needs, 204–207, 211–212; of resale responsibility, 147; for servicing needs, 145, 149–152
Overlap, employee, 12
Overmaintained equipment, 149
Overnight deliveries, reliance on, 100, 103, 104

P

Pareto charts, example of using, 44
Passive resistance, 18–19
Patient accounting department, 191–192
Patient referral, 112, 114–115
Patient satisfaction, 27, 33, 197
Patients: educating, 31–32; expectations of, 2; gifts to, 220; passing costs onto, 2; preregistering, 197–198; scheduling of, 26–27, 127, 132; underpayment by, *45*
Payers, third-party. *See* Third-party payers
Performance, job, 10–11, 12–13, 193
Perceived need: for equipment, 130–131, 158; for expansion, 177
Personal interviews, 54–55, 58, 69–70
Personal use of supplies, 223, 224
Phone service, 218–219
Physical plant operations, 180–181, 216, 217, 221–222

Physicians and providers: as customers, 24, 25; education and training for, 227–228; referral paths among, 131; scheduling of, 127, 132

Political agendas, 207

Positron emission tomography (PET) system, 115

Preregistration, importance of, 197–198

Preventive maintenance: emphasizing, 150, 159–161; leader in, 7

Pricing models, 83, 84–86, 87

Private and public insurers. *See* Third-party payers

Pro formas, using, 131, 139, 168, 178, 179, 192

Problem solving, creative. *See* Creative problem solving

Procedure value of services, addressing, 192–193

Process automation, vendors pushing, 46

Process improvement: critical areas for, 47–48; cutting cost with, 46–47; opportunities for, identifying, 59. *See also specific operations*

Process reengineering, 46, 132–134, 195

Production: control of, 103; cost of, validating, 86, 98

Production-based pricing models, 83, 85, *86*

Profit Line, 191

Project managers, 167

Project teams: training, 56–57; using, 147–148

Projected cash flow, predicting, 188

Projected growth, and expansion efforts, 177, 178

Projected utilization, 130–131

Projects, major. *See* Expansion projects

Prospective Payment System, 151

Providers. *See* Physicians and providers

Public and private payers. *See* Third-party payers

Public education, 32

Publix, 2, 7, 101

Purchase contracts: negotiation of, 99–100, 137, 182–183, 229–230; training in negotiating, 95, 96. *See also* Service contracts

Purchase planning. *See* Technology assessment; Utilization research and management

Purchase-avoidance tool, 127, 132–134

Purchasing: common mistakes in, 88–90, 145; for equipment service and repair, 153–156; during expansion process, 171–172, 181–183; issues in, overview of, 83–84; lessons on, 90–92; limits on, 18; pricing strategies in, 84–88; questions involving, 108–109; strategies for improving, 92–106; summary of, 107–108

Purchasing departments, 88, 95

Q

Quality and cost alignment: fact-finding process for, 41–45, 47–48; focus on, 7–8, 18, 37, 38; key to achieving, 46–48; lessons on, 48–49; overview of, 37; questions involving, 50–51; strategic planning for, 38–39; summary of, 49–50; testing for, 39–42

Quality and low cost: attaining, ability to, 18; leader in, 7

Quality breakers, 168

Quality control, 119; leader in, 7

R

Reagent costs, 120, 230

Real estate space, use of, 175–177

Rebates, problem with, 99

Record keeping, effective, 198–199

Recruiting, 67, 68

Recycling, 222–223

"Red-bag" problem, 222

Redeployment: of employees, 74–75; of equipment, 134, 157, 183

Redundancy: in education efforts, 228; in warehousing, 2, 100, 101; in work efforts, 12

Reentry points, 24

References, checking, 71

Referrals, 112, 114–115, 131